LIE
DETECTING
101

LIE DETECTING 101

A Comprehensive Course in Spotting Lies and Detecting Deceit

Dr. David Craig

Skyhorse Publishing

Caveat: The views and comments expressed in this book are solely the author's. The author does not represent any government agency, any commercial company or private body. The techniques contained in this book are utilized by lie-detection professionals around the world and when correctly applied, will improve the accuracy of lie detection in most people. However, no technique in lie detection is 100 percent accurate, and caution should be exercised before reaching a conclusion that a person has lied.

ACKNOWLEDGMENTS

I would like to thank my wife and four children for their support while I was committed to this project.

I would also like to acknowledge Denny Neave of Big Sky Publishing for his faith and commitment, and last but not least, Diane Evans, who provided insight and worked tirelessly to keep all the moving parts oiled and on time!

TABLE OF CONTENTS

INTRODUCTION

You were most likely attracted to this book because you are intrigued by the concept of knowing whether or not somone is telling you the truth, or you have unknowingly been lied to in the past and want to protect yourself against deception in the future. This book will assist you with both.

When I first began researching the subject of lie detection years ago, I realized that there were many high-level academic papers and textbooks on the subject, but no credible and easy-to-read guides offering knowledge and skills that could be put straight into practice—so I decided to write one.

If you are looking for a psychological edge when cutting a business deal, negotiating an outcome, interacting with people, or even making a purchase, then this book is for you. Lie detection does not have to be a sinister practice. You will find there are some fun and interesting exercises within these pages. Challenge your friends and family—can they get away with lying to you?

In addition to having over twenty years of criminological experience and research focused on deception and deception detection in covert operations, I have spent many hundreds of hours researching the theoretical work of some of the world's finest academics on this subject. The combination of theoretical knowledge and practical experience has enabled me to consolidate all the relevant information into a very practical book, which will quickly set you on the path to becoming a Human Lie Detector. Studies have shown that with training and practice most people can rapidly increase their success at detecting lies. This book will do this for you.

If your time is limited and you just want to get started, I have designed this book so you can bypass *Part One: Understanding Lies* and go straight to the practical section, *Part Two: Detecting Lies.* If you decide to start with the practical section, I recommend that, as you are practicing what you have read in *Part Two*, you make the time to read *Part One*, as it will provide you with a greater understanding of deception.

Knowing the difference between when people lie to you and when they are telling the truth is a vital human skill for the twenty-first century. Regardless of your age, gender, or background, this book will equip you with tools you need to become an effective Human Lie Detector. Happy hunting!

Part One

Understanding Lies

THE NATURE OF LYING

Mendacity, fib, untruth, falsehood, whopper, yarn—I've even heard it politely referred to by an American presidential candidate as having "misspoke." I'm not sure that's even a word—perhaps it was a lie. Regardless of the title or the context within which it occurs, we all have an opinion on what a lie is, and there are a multitude of different descriptions for the act of lying. In my opinion, a lie is a physical act, verbal statement, or omission, deliberately designed to deceive another of the truth. For example, a person could lie physically, as a shoplifter does, projecting the "physical" impression to store security of an honest shopper, while secretly removing goods from the shelves. Verbally, a person may attempt to deceive another person by saying, or not saying, particular words. Both examples are designed to deceive another of the truth.

Most people would agree that lying is an act of dishonesty, and it is this negative connotation that leads most people, when asked, to say they very rarely lie. In almost all cases, this is incorrect. There have been many independent academic studies on the frequency of lying in society. Some have revealed that people lie as little as twice a day (only 730 times a year!), whereas more recent research shows on average people lie three times in every ten minutes of conversation.[2] Robert Feldman's research found some middle ground when he conducted a study at the University of Massachusetts, which found that 60 percent of the people he researched lied at least once every ten minutes during conversation.[3] To most people these are surprising statistics, verging on unbelievable. This is understandable considering that one of the most offensive things a person can be called by another is a liar. The fact remains, however, that studies conducted across a variety of societal groups and cultures have revealed that while the frequency of lying may differ from study to study, lying is a universal and everyday event.

When people first hear this they disagree—and I admit that initially it sounds quite shocking. It is only through understanding the very nature of lying that these statistics make sense and it becomes easier to accept that lying is a very normal part of human interaction. Once you understand the nature of lying and can identify that someone has lied to you, you will be able to calculate the motivation behind why the person lied.

Broadly speaking there are two categories of lies: Self-Focused and Other-Focused. Self-Focused Lies are told to help the person telling the lie, whereas Other-Focused Lies are told to help another person. We'll examine the Other-Focused Lies first, as these are usually innocuous and are rarely hurtful or threatening. On the other hand, Self-Focused Lies do have the very real potential to detrimentally affect the people to whom they are told. That being the case, after a short discussion on the nature of Other-Focused Lies, the remainder of the book will examine in detail Self-Focused Lies and how you can detect them.

Other-Focused Lies

Other-Focused Lies are, as the name suggests, lies that are focused upon another person. They are usually told with good intentions, and, in most cases, if the truth is discovered it is not overly hurtful to the person to whom the lie was told. These lies are sometimes referred to as white lies or good-will lies, and the motivation for telling them is to benefit or protect another person in some way.

For example, you may meet a good friend you have not seen for many years and say to him, "You've barely changed since we last met." However, he might have put on weight, gained gray hair, and aged significantly more than you expected. Regardless, he is a good friend, and it's good to see him, so you wouldn't want to spoil this by coldly stating your real observations: "Wow, you've put on weight, your hair is definitely gray and thinning, and boy, you're looking old. Still, it's good to see you!" It might be the last time you see him; people don't always expect or want the truth.

Similarly, suppose a friend or colleague of yours has been very ill and has lost a shocking amount of weight and become very pale. Despite these observations, you may feel as though the person needs a lift, and you may tell one of the Other-Focused Lies by complimenting the person. Both of these examples are lies, Other-Focused Lies, but told for good reasons.

Other examples may include a father's feigned delight at receiving yet another set of socks on Father's Day, or the mother who thanks her four-year-old daughter for the tasty honey and sardine sandwich she made for her lunch.

Here are some example questions that may automatically evoke an Other-Focused Lie, for the benefit of the person asking the question:

- "Does my butt look big in this?"
- "Do you like my new shoes?"
- "Do you think I've put on weight?'"

Other-Focused Lies are also automatically told in response to frequently asked questions such as, "How are you?;" "How have you been?;" "How's the family?" On nearly all occasions when this question is asked, the response is an automated and positive Other-Focused Lie: "Fine;" "Not bad;" "Good." When this question is posed, unless it is a genuine welfare check, the person who is asking does not expect or want a fully detailed and accurate response. Consider a situation where two work colleagues pass each other in the office hallway. One says to the other, "Hi, how have you been—how's the family?" Imagine a totally honest response, "I'm all right, though I have a bit of a headache and these shoes are killing me. I keep worrying about the argument I had with my partner this morning, we seem to be drifting apart these days. Peter is doing well at school but he never seems to clean his room and it really annoys me."

Clearly, this question was asked as a polite symbolic statement to the other, to demonstrate an interest in the coworker as a person—though not interested enough to hear all the details, nor would the responder wish to share these details for reasons of privacy or not wanting to burden the other person with these problems. These types of questions are commonplace in most cultures and are usually responded to in the same positive and automated way.

Other-Focused Lies need not always be superficial or simply aligned with social etiquette, nor are they always practiced among friends or colleagues. Other-Focused Lies can also involve a significant degree of deception between total strangers, sometimes necessarily so. For example, consider a situation where a person witnesses a distressed wife fleeing her house and seeking refuge from her enraged husband in a neighbor's house. If questioned by the husband, it would be reasonable to expect the witness to tell an Other-Focused Lie to protect the wife, e.g. "I think she ran that way," indicating a false direction to the husband or denying seeing anything. The witness may not know any of the parties involved with the situation, but the principle of the Other-Focused Lie remains: a lie told for the benefit of, or to protect, another person—in this case the wife.

Society allows, and in fact, expects these types of lies to be told as a part of normal human interaction. This category of lie is the lubricant that keeps the wheels of social interaction turning smoothly, avoiding any unnecessary friction. Despite the usual "good will" motivating a person to tell an Other-Focused Lie, it remains most definitely a lie, as it is deliberately designed to deceive another of the truth. However, it's very hard to criticize someone who tells this type of lie, and in fact there is an expectation that most within society will do so.

Take a moment now to reflect upon the statistics in respect to the high frequency of lying that was stated earlier—is lying once in every ten minutes of conversation still so surprising? If you really want to test these statistics yourself, I suggest you keep a "Lie Diary" for one week, writing in it every time you lie, no matter how small the lie may be. If you are totally honest about your lies, you'll be surprised at how often you lie and how necessary lying is. If you're still unconvinced, try not lying for an entire week—this is extremely difficult, and you will likely offend people by always telling the truth.

Hopefully this section has provided you with some understanding as to why there is such a high frequency of lying, and also that it is not always a dishonorable act for a person to lie, particularly with Other-Focused Lies. The next category of lies, however, can carry a much more sinister agenda.

Self-Focused Lies

In contrast to Other-Focused Lies, Self-Focused Lies are told as a means of benefiting or protecting the person telling the lie. Studies have shown that 50 percent of lies told fall into this category.[4] There are four separate motivations for a person telling a Self-Focused lie to you. These are:

- To protect from embarrassment.
- To make a positive impression.
- To gain an advantage.
- To avoid punishment.[5]

I'll provide some examples so you can more easily recognize each of these forms of Self-Focused Lies when you encounter them.

To Protect from Embarrassment

This is the least harmful motivation for someone to tell a Self-Focused Lie. Examples may include:

- A reason is fabricated as to why someone can't meet for a drink, when in fact the real reason is that the person simply can't afford to.

- Though having spent the weekend alone, someone attests to having had a great weekend, simply to avoid the shame of not having had any company.

- When a person is asked why he or she is taking public transportation to work instead of driving, the person may say it is because it is hard to find parking in the city, rather than admitting that it is really because the person had a car accident and the car is getting repaired.

As you can see from these examples, the nature of this motivation for telling a Self-Focused Lie is understandable, though sometimes misunderstood; these lies are rarely hurtful or damaging.

To Make a Positive Impression

Wanting to make a positive impression is a very common factor in telling Self-Focused Lies. The motivating factor for wanting to tell a lie in order to impress someone is generally due to insecurities on the part of the deceiver, who feels the need to exaggerate beyond what is actually the truthful situation. There are varying degrees of fabrication under this category, from slight exaggeration to complete fabrication. On most occasions people will color the truth with a small degree of false information as a means to improve the way others perceive them. Less frequent, but with the potential to be more harmful, is the total fabrication of some aspect that the deceiver invents with the express purpose of impressing others.

This motivation can be present in situations such as when a couple first commences dating or where there is some perceived competition between two individuals or an individual and others, as may occur between adult siblings at a family gathering or former classmates at a school reunion. Some examples of these types of lies include:

- Exaggerating how much a person earns.
- Pretending to know celebrities or well-connected social identities (name dropping).
- Making up personal, or in some cases, one's child's academic qualifications, sporting achievements, or skills.
- Inflating the number of staff a person is responsible for supervising, or exaggerating the scope of a professional role or importance within a professional or sporting group.

The effect of this type of lie can vary from irrelevant false information that has no adverse effect, to the potential to undermine or destroy a relationship and cause a significant degree of personal hurt—as could be the case if a couple's relationship was formed on significantly false information. Within a business context, there is also the potential for monetary loss or professional embarrassment. For example, a CEO or business partner could be falsely led into agreeing to hire or to go into partnership with an under qualified deceiver, or negotiating a business outcome based upon misleading statements made by a deceiver—both could be costly mistakes for the business. These examples bear testimony as to why it is important to be able to detect liars in both business and personal interactions. The more sinister of "positive impression lies" could also in some cases fall within the following category: to gain an advantage.

To Gain an Advantage

As was previously discussed, when taken to the extreme, the motivation of wanting to create a positive impression can be harnessed with the ulterior motive of also wanting to gain an advantage. Lying to gain an advantage is clearly a sinister act and certainly worth identifying. Some examples include:

- Inventing circumstances where the deceiver requires someone's help, such as personal or financial assistance.
- Spreading false information about another person with whom he or she is in competition.
- Fabricating aspects of a job application or previous work history (very common).
- If selling, fabricating the history or worth of the object for sale.
- If buying, claiming to have less money or stating that a similar object is for sale at a cheaper price elsewhere in order to have the sale price reduced.

Within a social group, one person may initiate false rumors about another for the sole purpose of denigrating the other person's credibility. You may be the person targeted by such lies, in which case you have two courses of action: First, highlight the inconsistencies in the facts of the rumor with others in the group, which if done successfully will have the opposite effect to what the deceiver intended. Second, you could confront the people you suspect are responsible for initiating the rumor, and by utilizing your newly found lie-detection skills, quickly identify the culprit. In a similar circumstance, these skills may assist you in quelling a rumor if a deceiver attempts to provide you with false information about another person, as you will be able to quickly determine the truth of the situation.

Within a business context it is common for individuals or companies to try to gain an advantage. Sometimes this is through exaggerated information or outright lies by the individuals concerned. If you are doing business in a competitive industry where the ethos is "any advantage at any cost," it is highly likely that you or your company will be targeted by such falsehoods. As clever liars incorporate false information within genuine facts, having the ability to tell the difference between the two—particularly in respect to business negotiation where some information may be exaggerated and some discounted to create an advantage over you or your company—can protect your commercial interests. This book will examine in detail exactly how to identify false information, which with practice you will be able to do far more reliably than you can most likely do now.

To Avoid Punishment

Lying to avoid punishment is a very strong motivating factor in Self-Focused Lies and one that is quickly initiated by a person for self-protection or to avoid personal responsibility. As with all reasons for lying, there is a wide-ranging spectrum from minor to significant. The extent to which a person will lie to avoid punishment is usually directly proportional to the consequences of being caught—the greater the consequences, the more elaborate and extreme the lies will be in order to avoid the punishment. For example, a fabricated reason as to why a person is late for a meeting (e.g. traffic jam) with a friend or colleague may be offered quickly and without a lot of forethought, as the consequence of being found out is minor—just a degree of personal embarrassment. However, for a murderer being interviewed by the police, the fabricated alibi or cover story is often elaborate, detailed, and well-planned, as the consequences of being caught are significant. The examples listed below demonstrate varying degrees of severity in the lies told to avoid punishment:

- One child blaming another for writing on a wall or losing an item of clothing.
- A fabricated excuse offered to a parking enforcement officer.
- Damage to a motor vehicle, explained to a car owner, spouse, or an insurance provider by a complete denial of knowledge, such as the common excuse: "Another car must have run into it when I was parked at the mall."
- Falsification of business records to avoid tax responsibilities.
- A spouse or partner inventing an alibi while really having an affair.

The ramifications of a person successfully lying to you to avoid punishment may only be minor or could be quite damaging, as would be the case if the deceiver convinced you another person was to blame, and you in turn accused the innocent person.

Understanding the motivation behind lying is the first step in detecting a lie. When a person is giving you information, you should quickly be able to assess whether there is in fact any motivation for that person to lie to you. If there is, then you need to turn on your lie radar, or, as I like to call it, "Liedar," and start scanning for verbal signs (what the person says and how it is said) and nonverbal signs (what the person does/how the person acts). Additionally, if you suspect that a person has lied to you, understanding the categories and motivation behind the lie will provide you with insight into that person's mind and give you a psychological advantage when when you next interact with him or her. You will, from that point forward, have a far more effective ability to detect lies told by that person.

We have discussed the motivations behind Other-Focused Lies (usually told with a good intention by the deceiver) and the Self-Focused Lies (told to benefit or to protect the person telling the lie). There is not always a clear divide between these two categories. Understanding the motivation behind them will assist you to quickly differentiate between the two. For example, how do you answer when your boss asks, "Do you enjoy working here?" If your response is that you do enjoy working there when in fact you don't, this is most likely an Other-Focused Lie, designed to satisfy your boss. However, if your motivation for saying this was not to please your boss, but to gain favor with the boss, then this would be a Self-Focused Lie. Of course, you could also be telling the truth!

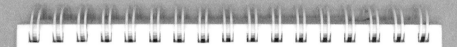

Summary of Main Points

Lying is a normal part of human communication and should not always be considered a bad thing to do.

People lie regularly, about once every ten minutes during conversation.

Sometimes lying is necessary to protect a person's feelings and to assist with everyday human interaction. On other occasions lying can be very detrimental to people and relationships.

Other-Focused Lies are directed at another person and are usually told by the deceiver with good intention. They are sometimes called white lies or good-will lies.

Self-Focused Lies may be directed at any person, but are told for the purpose of benefitting or protecting the person telling the lie. While not always the case, this category of lie can be detrimental.

THE NATURE OF LIE DETECTION: HOW GOOD ARE WE—NATURALLY?

Children learn from a very young age (around five years old) that they can attain knowledge that others don't have and therefore manipulate another's perception of fact. In other words, they learn to lie. Despite discovering this ability at a very early age, children are novice liars, and so their lies are quite easily detected by adults. However, as people continue through life telling Self-Focused and Other-Focused Lies for a variety of reasons, they become more accomplished in the art of deceiving others. Accepting that, in general, humans do lie regularly (often with good intentions) and therefore should be well-practiced at it, how good are we at detecting the lies that others tell us?

Most people over estimate their ability to detect lies. You're reading this book, which is aimed at teaching people how to detect lies, so perhaps you don't fit into this category. However, it is clear that most people are over confident when it comes to knowing when someone is lying. Most people believe that they can tell if their partner or close friend lies to them. Surprisingly, this is not generally the case. There are two primary reasons for this misunderstanding: confidence and closeness. Let me explain.

Due to the close relationship with the partner or close friend, a person "naturally" becomes over confident in being able to identify lies told by that person. This assumption is based upon the person's belief that he or she knows the partner more intimately than most, and will therefore be able to identify any telltale signs of deceit. This assumption is greatly weakened by the fact that humans inherently want to believe what they are told by those they love. Understandably, it is very difficult in an intimate relationship to remain objective and calculating in terms of assessing whether or not that person is lying. On one hand, people want to believe they are being told the truth, and on the other, they are over confident that they'll see it if it occurs, due to the closeness of the relationship. The combination of these two factors can lead a person in a relationship to overlook otherwise obvious signs—signs often detected by people outside the relationship.

As will be discussed in more detail later in the book, these skills must be practiced regularly to be an expert lie detector. It's unnatural for parents to continuously be suspicious of their children throughout the entirety of their childhood. Similarly, it is not conducive to a close relationship for one partner to continuously assess and be suspicious of the other. It is for these two reasons that people don't often focus their "Liedar" on those they love, and they are therefore at a disadvantage when they do because they are not well-practiced in looking for their partners'/ friends' telltale signs of deceit. Often others outside a relationship are better at detecting the lies of those involved within the relationship. Why? Because they don't have the close and confident factors to overcome, they remain objective and are therefore more accurate at assessing the verbal and nonverbal clues of lying.

Has there been a situation in your life where you have seen one partner lying to the other, and yet that partner seems to miss all the clues that are obvious you? Similarly, has there been a situation when you've heard a person in a relationship who has suffered because of a significant lie say, "I just didn't see it coming"? Perhaps after a relationship or friendship has ended, you have reflected on certain things and realized that perhaps the person wasn't as honest as you thought when you were in the relationship. The reason that you have better clarity to assess the degree of truthfulness of the person after a relationship has ended is because some of the confidence and closeness has been eroded or completely removed. It is often the case that after a relationship has ended, due to one partner's infidelity, the innocent party gains the objectivity to see there had been evidence of the infidelity during the relationship. The closeness and confidence hid them in plain view.

Many parents believe they can always tell when their children lie. This is true when their children are younger. However, as children become older they become better at lying, and by the time they reach the age of fifteen, lies can become extremely difficult to detect. Parents need to keep in mind that while they have had a lifetime of observing their children's behavior—including detecting lies, which is easy while they're younger (causing the parent to be over confident)— the child has also had a lifetime of observing the parents' behavior and has learned through experience every time they have successfully lied. Accordingly, children modify and develop their behavior. By the time they are adolescents they have a veritable database stored away on ways they have manipulated, harassed, or successfully lied to their parents to get what they want or to avoid punishment. I am by no means cynical of children or being critical in anyway. Everyone has gone through this process while growing up, and most would agree that they have manipulated or lied to their parents and got away with it at some stage during their childhood, more successfully so as a teenager.

All is not lost though, as parents will still be able to detect most lies told by their children regardless of age, where there is a high level of emotion attached to the lie. For example, the child may have done something significantly wrong and may feel an extreme amount of personal guilt or fear of the consequences (Emotional Response). When this occurs, the child's amplified emotion causes a Sympathetic Nervous Response and can trigger obvious telltale signs of lying, such as averting eye contact and fidgeting. (Emotional Response and Sympathetic Nervous Response are examined in *The Lying Response* on page 32). Regardless of how practiced children become at deceiving their parents, it is still very difficult for them to disguise a lie where there is a huge detrimental consequence or punishment for doing so. On the other hand, when children tell a small lie, they know their parents will not be extremely disappointed or overly angry if the lie is discovered. They know that this small betrayal, if discovered, won't end with a significant punishment. For these two reasons there is not a large degree of emotion attached to the lie, and there will only be extremely subtle deceit clues that will reveal the child has in fact lied.

Despite the fact that parents continually try to teach children to always tell the truth, there is a school of psychological thought that says it is natural for children to lie to their parents as part of gaining autonomy and independence as they grow up. This may be true; however, parents can take solace that they will, in most cases, always be able to tell when their children tell them a "whopper." Later, this book reveals some of the subtle secrets in astute lie detection that may assist parents when interacting with their children. If you are a parent, I advise you to hide this book from your children!

So, if most people over estimate how good they are at detecting lies, how good are we "naturally" at detecting lies—without training, special skills, and knowledge? Studies have shown that, despite our general over confidence we are in fact not very good at detecting lies.[6] In fact, most people have only a 50 percent chance of accurately identifying when someone has lied. This isn't because we lie perfectly; it has been found that 90 percent of lies are accompanied by detectable clues, both verbal and nonverbal.[7] Interestingly, research has found that there is no universal difference in the capacity to detect lying between genders, age, and social status.[8] Regardless of whether we are male or female, young or old, none of us are "naturally" very good lie detectors.

It appears strange that we seem to have an ongoing need and natural ability to regularly tell lies as part of our normal human interaction—sometimes understandably so and other times maliciously, or for self protection—and yet we are poor at detecting lies. This is even more peculiar when you consider that one of the highest values we place on personal relationships is honesty. It would be reasonable to assume that as we value honesty so highly we should be attuned to detect it (or the lack of it), and our capability to lie would be matched by an ability to detect lies as part of the evolutionary process. However, this is not the case.

Why, then, are we better at lying than detecting lies? Professor Paul Ekman, the person on whom the fictional television series character Dr. Cal Lightman of *Lie to Me* is based, puts forward some interesting evolutionary explanations for this phenomenon.[9] To summarize, Professor Ekman states that our ancestral environment, which consisted of small groups of people living in close proximity to each other with very little privacy, didn't prepare us to have to psychologically assess and detect whether someone was being truthful. For example, in the case of adultery being committed within a group, due to the lack of privacy it would likely be physically "discovered" or by chance witnessed by other members, rather than having been ascertained through psychological assessment. Professor Ekman also believes the ramifications of being caught telling a lie in those primitive times would have been severe, possibly ending in death. In such an environment, lies would not have been told very often because of the significant ramifications of being caught, and the chances of being caught were high due to the lack of privacy. It appears as though our evolutionary background has taught us that we don't need to try hard to catch a person lying because it will be "physically discovered," and that lying doesn't happen very often due to the serious consequences of doing so. Perhaps also it has taught us that when we do lie, we need to be very good at it.

In the twenty-first century, we live in a society where privacy is, quite rightly, vehemently protected and closely guarded. As such, the opportunity to "discover" or by chance witness another's deceitful act is significantly reduced. For example, consider the exponentially increasing number of cyber crimes where the victim of the crime, be it a person, bank, or institution, has no personal interaction with, or even sees the perpetrator. Not that long ago, a check fraud thief had to show his/her face in the bank or business when cashing a fraudulent check, providing at least an opportunity for bank staff to detect the deceitful behavior firsthand. Even bank robbers had the decency to at least visit the bank they were robbing! Today, credit card numbers can be stolen and personal bank funds may be transferred into a thief's bank account instantaneously— often via the encrypted laptop of some young cyber thief utilizing the free Wi-Fi of various businesses around the city, making the thief all but untraceable. In an effort to recover some of the funds, if a victim of such a crime then made enquiries into the transactions—where they occurred, who had access to the particular business Wi-Fi network etc.—the victim would very quickly find that all this information is protected by privacy policies and laws. Of course, these crimes can be investigated by law enforcement agencies that have the power to demand such information. I'm not an advocate against the protection of privacy (far from it), but these examples demonstrate the significance our society places on personal privacy, much more so than thousands of years ago. It appears things have changed greatly since our ancestors first walked the earth.

The ramifications of lying need not be as severe or long lasting as they were thousands of years ago. Today, liars who have previously been caught can easily change jobs, change partners, change phone numbers, change their "village," and even change their name to avoid the ongoing consequences of deceitful behavior. Even serious criminals (who often utilize deceit as a business tool) are well supported by twenty-first century justice and rehabilitation policy. Court orders often suppress publication of their names and allow them to change their names upon release in order to make a fresh start, free from any consequences of their previous deceit. These examples are not provided to be critical of rehabilitation policies, but to highlight the ways in which our society is now more conducive to telling lies; there are more opportunities and less ramifications. Now more than ever we need to have astute lie-detection skills. Clearly, twenty-first century humans need to evolve and evolve quickly.

We come from an evolutionary background where lying didn't occur very often, and when it did we had to be good at it. The detection of lying wasn't often required, so it is understandable why today we find the "mental arms race" between lying and being able to detect lies "naturally" won by the former. Thanks, Doctor Darwin.

Gaining additional knowledge and practical skills to strengthen your lie-detection arsenal can redress this evolutionary imbalance. You are doing it right now by reading this book. By gaining additional theoretical knowledge and applying this practically, it is possible to attain rates as high as 80 percent accuracy in lie detection. Hopefully, by the end of this book you will be well on your way becoming a Human Lie Detector.

In summary, due to the evolutionary process there is a vast imbalance between our ability to tell lies and our poor ability to detect them. However, you will be able to dramatically improve and develop your ability to detect lies by gaining additional knowledge and practice. This will give you a mental advantage when interacting with others who are "naturally" less accustomed to looking for lies in everyday conversation. In the twenty-first century, it is advantageous in personal, business, and general human interactions to have the psychological skills to assess degrees of truthfulness in others. You are well on your way.

While this book is focused upon increasing personal lie-detection skills, I don't suggest you keep your "Liedar" turned on at all times. It is my view that people are generally good, and that while we lie frequently as we make our way through life, most lies are harmless. I believe it is neither healthy nor desirable for a person to take a constant doubting and suspicious stance toward everyone. To do so would have two adverse effects: First, it would foster a more cynical outlook on life and make it difficult to find intimacy and enjoy trusting relationships; and second, accuracy in lie detection would also falter. Studies have shown one of the primary factors inhibiting investigators from making accurate assessments of deceit is that they commonly approach suspects with the view that the suspect is guilty, and they just need to find proof. This bias clouds their objective assessment, and they miss vital nonverbal clues. On the other hand, a more accurate lie detector will approach each person from a purely objective viewpoint and assess both verbal and nonverbal behaviors for clues of deception in a measured and unclouded way.

Additionally, I believe you will be far more focused and effective when you do turn on your "Liedar" if you are not looking for lies all the time. While I don't believe you need to have your "Liedar" on at all times, it can be an extremely vital tool (when required) to protect yourself or others you care about in business and personal relationships. Judgement just needs to be shown as to when you want to hit the "on" switch.

We have established that "naturally," we are not very good at detecting lies; certainly not as good as we think we are. Perhaps this is understandable for the layperson, but what about the people in our society—such as police, judges, lawyers, and psychiatrists—who have a vested interest in having a high lie-detection rate? Surprisingly, two reliable and independent studies of these specific categories revealed that these professionals were only able able to detect lies 50 percent of the time.[10] In fact, a comprehensive study conducted by Kraut and Poe found that US Customs Officers were no more accurate in detecting deceit than college students.[11]

The study by Professors Paul Ekman and Maureen O'Sullivan found that after testing secret service agents, federal polygraphers, investigators, judges, psychiatrists, and college students, there was one group that outperformed all the others.[12] The majority of those tested achieved between 40–60 percent accuracy. As was discussed earlier, this is approximately the accuracy expected of a person "naturally." However, more than half of the US Secret Service officers tested achieved above 70 percent accuracy.

One of the explanations as to why this group outperformed all others was that they were involved in close personal protection (bodyguard) duties, protecting important government officials. In this role, these guards are constantly scanning crowds in an effort to identify suspicious behavior that may lead to a threat against the person they're protecting. By constantly observing the behavior of others and focusing their minds upon detecting threat clues, it appears as though they have developed an ability to detect nonverbal deceit. In short, they have developed an ability to identify guilt or at least deceptive behavior through observation skills. I have had the opportunity to undertake similar roles and can attest from my first-hand experience that after a period of constantly assessing people, there is a noticeable increase in the capacity to rapidly make an assessment of a person's intention based on observation of his or her nonverbal behavior.

The ability to assess nonverbal behavior can greatly increase the accuracy of lie detection. Studies have shown that people who are trained in detecting lies use different tactics to do so than people who are less accurate in detecting lies. The primary difference is that accurate lie detectors observe a combination of verbal and nonverbal behavior to make their assessment. Inaccurate lie detectors place a greater emphasis on verbal information alone; they rely on what they are told to establish whether someone is lying. Accurate lie detectors rely on a combination of what they're told and what they observe.[13]

There have been a multitude of books written on body language, some by well-credentialed academics and professionals, and some by others less qualified. Regardless, one common thread that ties most of these publications together is that they all believe that nonverbal behavior (what is done) has more influence on communication than verbal (what is said). There have been a variety of different studies conducted to estimate the proportion of verbal versus nonverbal percentages during human communication. Some have placed nonverbal communication as high as 80 percent, though I find this questionable. A more realistic result, which has subsequently been supported by other studies, was found when Albert Mehrabian was conducting extensive research into body language. Mehrabian found that 55 percent of communication was nonverbal (how the body moves), 38 percent was vocal (how things are said), and only 7 percent was purely verbal (what is said).[14] Based on this and other research it is clear that people rely more on nonverbal behavior (55 percent) than on verbal behavior (45 percent) in respect to communication. Does the same hold true in respect to lie detection?

As mentioned before, the US Secret Service personnel rated above all others tested in respect to lie-detection accuracy, and one of the reasons for this was their well-practiced and accurate interpretation of nonverbal behavior. Reinforcing this concept was a study that compared people suffering from Aphasia with healthy individuals. Aphasia is a condition caused by damage to the left hemisphere of the brain that results in the total or partial loss of ability to understand spoken or written language. This study pitted the Aphasic group, who have no understanding of what words in a sentence mean, and therefore must rely totally on voice tone and nonverbal behavior, against a group who have normally functioning brains.

The healthy group in their assessment would logically listen to what was said and how it was said and also observe nonverbal behavior. The Aphasics could only perform the latter two tasks, as they simply could not understand what was said. Surprisingly, the research found that the Aphasics outperformed the other group significantly in detecting lies.[15] The Aphasics clearly relied upon what they saw in the person's behavior and how the words were said to identify who was lying. This removes any doubt that, while logically what is said is important, it is not as important as how it is said, nor is it as important as observing the person's nonverbal behavior as the person speaks.

Perhaps this also gives us a clue as to why judges performed averagely in the previously mentioned test. In court, evidence is provided in the form of photographs, written statements, forensic re-creations, and the oral testimonies of people who are sworn to tell the truth. In addition, from an evidentiary perspective, a court is primarily interested in what is said, not how things are said. How something is said is not evidence, nor is someone's nonverbal behavior while giving evidence, although it may go against a person's credibility to look guilty in the eyes of the jury (and judge) while giving the testimony. Therefore, it is perhaps understandable why judges pay particular attention to exhibits produced before them and also to exactly what is said before them rather than how something is said or the nonverbal behavior of the person while speaking. Despite what personal views a judge may form about a witness or a defendant, professionally, judges are predominantly concerned with facts, and this forms the focus of their assessment. This being the case, they are not well-practiced at assessing whether someone is telling the truth based upon nonverbal behavior. This provides a reasonable explanation as to why judges did not perform as well in the test as most would expect.

So, we have established that without specific lie-detection training, everyday citizens and professionals are not very good at detecting lies. However, there is one very small group within our community that is the exception to the rule— Lie Wizards.

Lie Wizards constitute a very small group in society and have the ability to detect lies with a high degree of accuracy. As previously discussed, the average person has the ability to detect lies with around 50 percent accuracy. With training and practice this accuracy level can be raised to about 80 percent accuracy. Lie Wizards, however, have a natural accuracy rate of 80 percent or better, with no training whatsoever. They are extremely rare though, as approximately only two in every one thousand people have this ability.[16] Dr. O'Sullivan conducted an extensive study into lie-detection wizards and found that this group was made up equally of both men and women from varying educational backgrounds. This is encouraging, as it proves that gender and education levels are irrelevant to one's ability to detect lies.[17]

There are a number of theories about why these people have such a naturally high degree of accuracy. These theories range from the Lie Wizard growing up in a dysfunctional or violent household where the identification of threats through nonverbal communication became highly developed as a child, to a skill developed from childhood by the constant study of people's faces and reactions either by a natural inherent motivation or through some form of interest such as drawing or sketching portraits. Regardless of how this ability was attained, the findings in most studies show that the detection by these Lie Wizards is based primarily via nonverbal clues, most commonly facial. It appears as though members of this select group have a highly developed ability to detect micro-expressions and other very subtle signs that are lost on us mere mortals. Micro-expressions are expressions demonstrating an emotion that appears extremely briefly (1/25 of a second) on a person's face. These are discussed in more detail in the following chapter on page 84.

There is no conclusive evidence identifying that Lie Wizards were born with this ability; rather, they learned and developed their skills over a long period of time. Dr. O'Sullivan found that Lie Wizards are motivated. They want to get things right, and they practice their skills constantly, like athletes.[18] This should provide you with some encouragement, as it further validates that knowledge and practice do in fact increase the ability to detect lies.

If you are already a Lie Wizard, then this book won't be of great benefit to you. However, if you want to become a Lie Wizard, then intensive study and practice over a period of time will set you on the correct path. Lie Wizards are extremely rare. I'm pretty confident, though, that all my schoolteachers have been, in fact, Lie Wizards. They just seemed to know every time I did something wrong. They blamed me for everything I did, which seemed grossly unfair at the time! If you are unlucky enough to have a Lie Wizard for a child, then you can probably drop the whole Santa and Easter Bunny ruse; though you may want to invite them to assist you at your next poker game!

Other-Focused Lies: Told with good intention—"Does my butt look big in this?"

Self-Focused Lies: Told to protect from embarrassment—"I'm having a great birthday party. Everyone's here."

Self-Focused Lies: Told to make a good impression—"My other car's a Lamborghini."

Self-Focused Lies: To gain advantage—"Yes I've had a lot of experience in this industry."

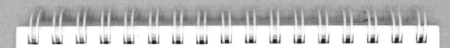

Summary of Main Points

Naturally, we are far better at telling lies than detecting them. Without specific training, most people, including those from professions where detecting lies is crucial, achieve a lie-detection rate of about 50 percent.

With specific knowledge (provided by this book), and practice (provided by you), people may achieve a lie-detection rate of 80 percent.

The more you use your "Liedar" the more accurate your lie-detection skills will become. However, you don't want it on constantly—knowing when to turn it on will make you more focused when you do use these skills.

There is a special category of Human Lie Detector (referred to as Lie Wizards) that has a natural talent in accurate lie detection without specific training, achieving starting percentages of 80 percent or better.

Most people believe that they can tell if their partner, child, or close friend lies to them. This is usually not the case, due to two primary factors: over-confidence (they know the person well and will therefore be able to see the telltale signs) and closeness (the natural default position for humans is to believe the people they are emotionally close to). These two factors lead to a loss of objectivity, which prevents a person in a close relationship from seeing otherwise obvious signs of deceit.

Studies have demonstrated that 55 percent of communication is nonverbal (how the body moves/reacts), 38 percent is vocal (how things are said) and only 7 percent is purely verbal (what is said). While what is said cannot be totally discounted in lie detection, how things are said and how a person's body moves/reacts while communicating are far more important.

Relying solely on what is said is inherently unreliable. Accurate lie detectors rely on a combination of what they're told and what they observe.

Part Two

Detecting Lies

If you have completed reading *Part One* you will now have a good understanding of the nature and motivation for lying. Now, *Part Two* will provide you with some additional theoretical knowledge before moving on to the practical aspects of lie detection—the fun stuff!

If you have skipped *Part One* and just started reading, then *Part Two* will provide you with some very basic but essential theory before moving on to the purely practical aspects of lie detection. In *Part One*, we discussed the need to be able to quickly assess whether there is any motivation for a person to lie to you when they are giving you information. If there is, then you need to turn on your lie radar, or, as I term it, "Liedar," and start scanning for verbal signs (what the person says and how it is said and nonverbal signs (what the person does/how the person acts).

If you suffer from chronic impatience (as I do), try to resist going directly to the *Lying Signs* section in *Part Two*, as the theory leading up to that section will greatly enhance your ability to improve your accuracy as a Human Lie Detector.

THE LYING RESPONSE

After a person tells a lie there is a series of responses. Some of these responses are nervous and automated, while some are consciously initiated by the person telling the lie to cover the deceit. Having an understanding of these responses will assist you greatly in identifying the deceit clues a person consciously or subconsciously exhibits when lying.

Broadly speaking, there are three responsive phases after a lie is told:
• Phase One: Emotional Response.
• Phase Two: Sympathetic Nervous Response.
• Phase Three: Cognitive Response.

Phase One: Emotional Response

When individuals tell a lie, they enter the phase of Emotional Response: recognition of what they have just done. If the lie is a minor one, or the person telling the lie has told that lie on a number of occasions and got away with it, or the person is an accomplished liar, there will only be a minor degree of Emotional Response. As a result, the following two responses (phases two and three) are very minor indeed. Under these circumstances it is difficult, though not impossible, to detect the lie. However, where individuals tell a significant lie, or one that they have not practiced, or one that has major ramifications for the liar if detected, there is a significant degree of Emotional Response. Feelings of guilt, fear, stress, and on occasion, excitement will manifest due to the liar's recognition of what he or she has just said and the consequences of that act. In these circumstances, the liar moves very quickly into phase two.

Phase Two: Sympathetic Nervous Response

The Sympathetic Nervous Response is, as the name suggests, the reaction of the nervous system to the Emotional Response phase. If the liar is emotionally charged with guilt, fear, stress, or excitement from the lie, his or her nervous system will also react, following the natural human "fight or flight" instinct. Instinctively, the liar's body responds by releasing adrenaline, which may manifest itself in ways that can be observed by the Human Lie Detector, sometimes referred to as "deceit clues." Obvious physical examples of these include finger tapping, fidgeting, talking too quickly, and rapid eye movement. When the liar enters this phase, your "Liedar" screen should be well and truly focused on that person.

Phase Three: Cognitive Response—a Counter-measure

The Cognitive Response is the liar's recognition of the manifestation of the Sympathetic Nervous Response. It is a mental and physical counter-measure, aimed at disguising the signs liars think will give them away. For example, in response to recognizing they are nervously fidgeting or have shaky hands, liars will attempt to exert some control over these deceit clues by disguising them. They may attempt to do this by holding a pen or hiding their hands out of sight, such as in their pockets or under a desk. These are rudimentary counter-measures and ones that should have your "Liedar" alarm beeping away.

Liars are usually aware of the most obvious signs that they are displaying and will attempt to control them. Unfortunately for liars, the ability to control these deceit clues is limited by their cognitive ability to self-monitor the changes in their own behavior. Some signs of lying are more easily controlled and monitored by the liar than others. For example, the previous case of fidgeting is one that is easily monitored and controlled by the liar in an attempt to hide that particular "deception clue." There are other signs of lying that can be very difficult for liars to monitor and control, such as the size of their pupils, increased rate of breathing, or a shaky voice.

The reason for this can be explained by the body's numerous nervous behavioral channels that conduct information to and from the brain. A channel that has a high sending and receiving capacity makes it easier for the liar to monitor and control that particular behavior. This is a highly conductive channel, one where the information to and from the brain flows freely and quickly, providing the liar with adequate feedback and allowing a significant degree of control over that deception clue. For example, the movement of fingers is a very repetitious behavior during day-to-day, living and as such, is a well-practiced (and therefore highly conductive) channel and one that provides liars with a high degree of control—hence liars hiding their hands, or holding on to a desk or pen to hide that giveaway clue. In short, liars recognize that their behavior has changed, and they have started to move their fingers more rapidly than they would normally. Then they use their Cognitive Response to slow that movement down, or to hide the movement completely, sometimes by grasping on to the arms of a chair or table.

The nervous behavioral channels have varying degrees of "conductivity." At the other end of the spectrum from the previous example are channels with little or no conductivity at all, which provide liars with little feedback and no control over disguising the changes in behavior when they have lied. For example, one of the signs a person is lying is an increase in the size of the pupils (pupil dilation). People don't often (if ever) attempt to control the size of the pupils, as this is a very unpracticed channel, lacking conductivity and one that does not provide very much control. As such, while not always practical (unless captured on film) this is one of the good signs to look for if someone is lying, as it is nearly impossible for the liar to hide this from you.

In short, nervous behavioral channels that provide the free flow of information quickly allow liars to control the "deception clue" more easily, whereas channels with less conductivity prevent them from accurately monitoring changes in their behavior, after they have told a lie.

As a Human Lie Detector, you shouldn't discount deceit clues from highly conductive channels such as fingers, hands, and the speed and quality of speech, but your primary focus will be on areas with less conductivity, such as the lower parts of the body, eye movement, and micro-expressions. (These are explained in more detail on page 84.)

The reason we keep monitoring, rather than discounting, the deceit clues from a highly conductive channel (such as finger movement) is that regardless of how efficient and conductive these channels are, under the right circumstances these too can become difficult for the liar to monitor. The reason for this is that the liar attempts to monitor all channels and control all possible deceit clues, while also attempting to maintain a convincing and logical verbal conversation. To do this causes a vast increase in the cognitive load on the brain (brain drain).

This can lead to a breakdown of the liar's control, which may see an otherwise easily controllable deception clue "leak" and become obvious. This is because humans only have a certain amount of brainpower and can only undertake a limited number of tasks simultaneously.

We can think of this mechanism in monetary terms. Consider that humans have $100 worth of brain capacity at any particular time. Liars need to spend this money carefully to avoid being detected. An example:

- $5 is spent on routine matters unrelated to the lie, such as responding to noises, thirst, and body temperature.

- $5 may be spent on ensuring they don't blink too often.

- $10 may be spent on controlling hands and arms.

- $10 may be spent on controlling the lower parts of the body.

- $10 may be spent to ensure they look the accuser in the eye sincerely.

- $10 may be spent on controlling how quickly they speak and how they speak.

- $10 may be spent on stressful thoughts associated with the consequences if they are caught lying.

- $40 needs to be spent on processing the information received from a question and formulating a credible false response to cover the lie.

TOTAL = $100

These amounts will vary depending upon the circumstances and the individual involved. The above example highlights that the brain is using 100 percent of its concentration. If this person is questioned at length and has to recall previous lies while also constantly manufacturing new information to fit in with previous false information told to cover the lie, the liar would need to add to the $40 account. Considering that there is only $100 worth of concentration, the money must be transferred from somewhere else, and this occurs to the detriment of the other channel.

For instance, a liar is asked a particularly difficult question, one that is very difficult to respond to quickly and naturally, so the $40 worth of concentration is not enough. The liar then looks down and focuses on an object to buy some time to think before responding with the answer. What has actually happened is that the liar has hit cognitive overload; there is a "zero balance" in the $40 account. The liar needs to balance the accounts by transferring $10 from the "ensuring they look the accuser in the eye sincerely" account, to make sure there is enough cash left to formulate an appropriate verbal response. This reveals two things to the lie detector: first, that person has stopped engaging in sincere eye contact (a "deception clue"), and secondly, there has been a significant pause before the liar responds to the question (another "deception clue"). Innocent people, because they don't need to monitor the various channels, may have as much as $80 worth of concentration available to process received information from a question and to formulate an appropriate response. The responses of a person telling the truth appear smooth and natural because cognitive overload is not being reached. There is a healthy balance in all accounts—proving that telling the truth is a good investment!

The more an individuals lie (answering a number of questions), the more they have to concentrate on what they are saying, and consequently, the less they are able to self-monitor and self-control. If they concentrate wholly on self-monitoring and controlling nonverbal clues, they will not be able to maintain a convincing verbal lie, and it will either not make logical sense or sound unconvincing, as they have reached mental overload.

Dramatic representations of mental overload are often seen in Hollywood crime movies, where detectives ask the suspect a series of hard-hitting questions in quick succession. This increases the pressure to such a degree that the suspect can no longer go on lying and makes admissions or confesses. While this occurs fictitiously in "movie land," the principle of what is being demonstrated functions in real life as well. The suspect cannot answer a number of questions quickly in a natural way (as each needs to be fabricated) and appear innocent by controlling body movement, because the cognitive load is too much. The suspect becomes mentally bankrupt.

When attempting to detect if an individual is lying, you may want to ask the person a number of questions and see if you can cause bankruptcy! If you can, the information the person provides verbally will be illogical. The subject will either not make sense or will exhibit obvious lying signs, such as fidgeting, abruptly changing the subject, or having an extended pause before replying.

The Lying Response

Phase 1. The Emotional Response.

Recognition of the consequences of lying. The liar experiences guilt, fear, stress, and occasionally excitement. There are few visual signs in this phase.

Phase 2. The Sympathetic Nervous Response.

The body in "fight or flight" mode. The nervous system reacts to the guilt and shows a cluster of "deceit clues"—eye contact is broken, one leg starts to shake, and the fingers start to tap.

Phase 3. The Cognitive Response.

A counter-measure designed to hide the lying signs. The hands hold the table to hide fidgeting, the ankles are locked and braced against the chair to stop movement, and eye contact is resumed.

Phase 1.

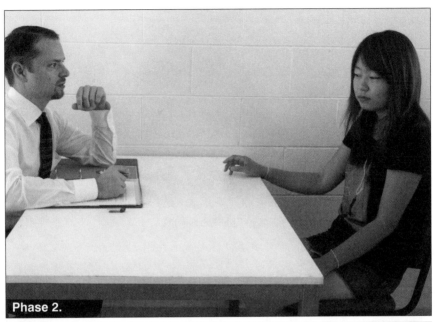

Phase 2.

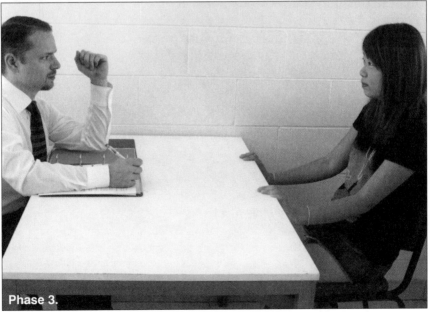

Phase 3.

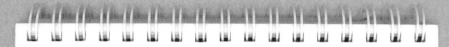

Summary of Main Points

Broadly speaking, there are three responsive phases after a lie is told:

Phase One: Emotional Response: The liar's recognition of his or her falsehood, which leads to feelings of guilt, fear, stress, and on occasion excitement. How great an impact this will have on the person and his or her behavior is predominantly determined by the magnitude of the consequences of being caught. For example, a small lie will only have a small amount of emotion attached to it. A major deception, such as infidelity, crime, or lying to secure a business contract or employment, will usually result in a noticeable increase in these emotions, making them easier to detect.

Phase Two: Sympathetic Nervous Response: The impact of guilt, fear, stress ,or excitement on the liar, which results in "deceit clues," such as finger tapping, fidgeting, talking too quickly, avoiding eye contact, and rapid eye movement.

Phase Three: Cognitive Response: A counter-measure attempt by the liar to cover up the "deceit clues." This is more easily done using highly conductive channels (areas of the body over which the liar easily maintains control i.e. hands and eye contact). These areas shouldn't be discounted. However, concentrating on areas with less control such as pupil size, lower body movements, and micro-expressions will be more productive.

The lying response sequence: If the Emotional Response is fear (phase one), and this causes the liar to tap their foot (phase two), the person will attempt to hide the leg movement (under a table or bracing the legs) to disguise guilt (phase three).

Consider that humans have $100 worth of brain capacity at any particular time. Liars need to spend this money carefully to avoid being detected. If they invest too much in hiding deceit clues revealed through body movement, their explanation will not make logical sense. Conversely, if the answer makes sense, they may not have invested enough in hiding guilty body movement. If you ask for further clarification you may be able to cause mental bankruptcy, revealing an array of obvious deceit clues.

LIE-DETECTION PROCESS—IT'S MAGIC!

Most people have some idea about what indicates that a person may be lying, for example fidgeting, sweating, and losing eye contact. While these are valid symptoms of a person lying, having only a base level of knowledge in respect to lie detection can lead to highly inaccurate conclusions. For example, as we have discussed, increased eye contact can also be a sign of lying—people know they have lied and are attempting to appear sincere. So the knowledge of or assumption that less eye contact is an iron-clad indicator of lying would lead to an incorrect lie detection. This lack of accurate knowledge can lead not only to suspecting innocent people of lying, but also to liars being assessed as innocent. Unfortunately, in respect to the subject of lie detection, it is true that a small amount of knowledge can be dangerous!

This is one of the main reasons for my writing this book. If people are interested in becoming a Human Lie Detector, I would like to give them the best opportunity to be as accurate as possible. No doubt you are aware of how unpleasant it is to be accused of something you haven't done. To avoid wrongly convicting others, it is important that we apply a rigorous but simple process when detecting lies. This strategy will increase your accuracy and the reliability of your detections.[19] I have broken the process down into five basic stages to create the MAGIC Lie Detection Model, an easy-to-remember lie-detection process that may be applied to all situations. A summary of the MAGIC Lie Detection Model and its application can be found at the back of the book. The five stages of the model are:

1. **M**otivation: Does the person have a motivation to lie?

2. **A**sk Control Questions: To establish a behavioral baseline.

3. **G**uilt Questions: Ask Guilt Questions.

4. **I**ndicators: Are there lying indicators in clue clusters?

5. **C**heck Again: Re-examine.

By combining these simple steps together with your knowledge of the lying signs (covered in the following section: *Lying Signs*), you will be well on your way to becoming an accurate Human Lie Detector.

Step 1: Motivation

Assess whether the person has a motivation to lie. As we previously discussed, motivations to lie include: to protect from embarrassment, to make a positive impression, to gain an advantage, and to avoid punishment. You'll be more accurate if you remain objective, so it's important to keep in mind that even if it seems as though the person has the motivation to lie, he or she could still be telling the truth. Regardless, this is an important step, particularly if you identify "to gain an advantage" or "to avoid punishment" as a motivation to lie, as this could result in harmful lies being told.

Step 2: Ask Control Questions—Establish a Behavioral Baseline

One of the reasons that lie detection is not an exact science and is difficult to undertake with a high degree of accuracy is the vast number of variances in human behavior in any given circumstance. For example, one of the common traits that indicate someone is lying is the inability to maintain eye contact. This can be true. However, in some cultures, liars will "naturally" increase the amount of eye contact. Additionally, if a person does maintain eye contact, it doesn't necessarily indicate innocence. As discussed earlier, this could be a deliberate counter-measure to simply project innocence. Adding more uncertainty, avoiding eye contact is also a normal behavior for some personality traits (e.g., shy, nervous, or insecure). Furthermore, the circumstance itself may cause the person to avoid eye contact, as can be the case when there is a significant authoritative disparity between two people, such as a teacher and a young child. In this circumstance, regardless of whether a child is innocent or not, holding the gaze of his or her teacher is a difficult thing to do.

So, is it necessary to understand every personality type and every expected cultural reaction for all given situations to detect lies? Absolutely not. There is a much simpler and more accurate way. When you turn on your "Liedar" to determine if a person is lying, the first thing you must do is establish a behavioral baseline. To establish an individual's behavioral baseline, you need to observe your subject's verbal and nonverbal responses to questions you know the answer to or which you know the subject will answer honestly. These are called Control Questions.

As the person is answering these Control Questions in a truthful way, you should observe (and remember) a number of his or her behaviors. Then you manipulate the conversation to an area where you feel the person may be lying and observe the behavioral characteristics again. At this point you make a comparison between the verbal and nonverbal behavior in response to questions the person answered truthfully against the responses to questions which you feel may have been answered untruthfully. If you identify changes in any of the lying clues (discussed in more detail below), then you may be on the path to identifying if the person is lying, or certainly an area that requires more probing.

Polygraph operators have used Control Questions for many years. The polygraph or lie detector machine is physically attached to the person being questioned and monitors physiological activity such as heart rate, breathing patterns, and Galvanic Skin Response (GSR), which includes sweat gland activity. Effectively, the polygraph monitors the subject's response to questions. The operator asks Control Questions—ones they already know the answers to, such as the person's name, gender, and address. As this is occurring, the operator observes graphs on the machine that are recording the physiological responses. Then the operator will move on to asking direct questions pertaining to suspicious activity the subject may have been a part of and look for a change in the physiological responses being recorded by the polygraph. If there is a significant contrast between the responses to known truthful answers and suspected lies, the operator will conclude the person is lying.

I don't believe a polygraph is a highly accurate lie detector, as there are some very simple tactics that can be used to defeat it. However, the process that has been adopted during a polygraph examination is valid, and one we should replicate as Human Lie Detectors. The first step in this process is to establish a behavioral baseline (based on Control Questions) and contrast these responses against responses to suspected untruthful answers.

To establish a behavioral baseline you simply need to ask the person questions you know the answer to, or to which the person would logically answer truthfully. While you are doing this, you observe the deceit clues, such as eye contact, blink rate, and hand movements. It's really worthwhile to spend some time establishing a solid behavioral baseline, so when you do ask questions where you suspect the person may lie, a change in the response will be very obvious to you. So it's best to take your time asking questions and observing.

Subtle Control Questions that fit naturally within a conversation are the best, so the person doesn't realize it's a test. For instance, you could ask, "Are you still living at Johnsonville?" or, "Are you still driving the white Toyota?" (when you know the person is). I also recommend asking the person to recall situations when you were present so you can judge the accuracy of the answer. For example, "Remember when we went to the tavern, was it there you first met Mike?" or, "Jenny, remember the office party for Robert—can you recall where you got the cake from?" This is an ideal question if "Jenny" was responsible for purchasing the cake, as she will recall this accurately and presumably be able to visualize the event. As discussed in the *Eye Movement* section on page 62, observing individuals' eyes can indicate whether they are recalling an event or fabricating an event. As such, a question like this will cause them to recall accurately what occurred, and you can observe their eye movement.

It's best to ask your Control Questions within a set period of time, such as at one meeting, party, or business lunch. This way there will be consistency in the mental state of the person and the responses. It is less reliable to ask Control Questions over several days, as the person's mental state, external distractions, and your memory are all vulnerable to change. Your Control Questions don't all have to be asked within quick succession either—just within the same environment that you plan to ask the Guilt Questions—allowing a reliable contrast to be drawn.

I really encourage people to be patient and take time to establish a reliable behavioral baseline, as this is the first critical step towards accurate lie detection and a good investment of your time—it will make signs of lying much more obvious to you.

Step 3: Guilt Questions—Ask the Guilt Questions

When you feel you have observed the person's responses to a number of Control Questions, it's time to move on to the juicy stuff! To identify a liar, you need to first provide the opportunity to lie. To do this you need to ask questions that provide the person with the opportunity to answer truthfully or to lie—it's the person's choice. To be an effective Human Lie Detector, you need to feel comfortable asking questions and be able to ask the questions in a natural way so they form part of a normal conversation.

If individuals suspect you are asking questions in an effort to identify their guilt, they will be able to initiate a type of counter-measure in an attempt to hide their guilt, such as ensuring they maintain eye contact. You don't want to provide them with an opportunity to put their defenses up, so it's best to ask questions as part of a normal conversation. Sometimes this won't be possible or desirable, and you may, after establishing a reliable baseline, choose to ask quite direct questions or challenge the person outright.

Keep in mind that when challenging people, even if they are innocent, they will change their behavior in response to a challenge; this may not indicate guilt, but rather that they are feeling defensive or antagonized because their integrity is being challenged. As such, it is best to subtly ask questions about which you feel a person is lying while continuing to look for signs of deceit. However, if you choose to challenge the person, take into account the possibility that some of the change in behavior may not be a direct result of guilt. Taking this into account, if you have taken the time to establish a reliable baseline and observe relevant lying signs, you will still be able to identify the difference between a person being defensive and a person being guilty.

In my opinion, an intelligent strategy after having identified someone is lying, is to make sure you act as though you haven't caught on. This strategy prevents liars from modifying their behavior when next you speak with them—it prevents them from commencing counter-measures, as they feel they can lie to you at will. Having the capacity to reliably identify when a person is lying may give you a future mental advantage or additional protection.

Step 4: Indicators—Are There Lying Indicators in Clue Clusters?

Because there is such a wide range of circumstances and personality traits across humanity, there is no single deception clue that can be relied upon to accurately identify if a person has lied. To be an accurate Human Lie Detector, it is best to look for "clusters" of deceptive signs rather than for an individual sign. To rely upon a singular sign can be highly inaccurate and result in an undesirable outcome. For example, it was mentioned previously that pupil dilation (pupils enlarged) could be a sign of lying. However, pupil dilation can occur for a number of reasons, including feelings of pleasure and attraction. It would be most unfortunate if a reader of this book decided that increased pupillary size by itself was a dead giveaway; particularly if the reader's partner came home with a bottle of wine, was looking forward to a romantic night, and said "I love you" (while demonstrating dilated pupils), only to be accused of lying by the misguided Human Lie Detector. So much for a romantic night!

It's much safer to look for a cluster of clues: a group of deceit clues that occur in quick succession. When this occurs in response to a question, your "Liedar" should activate.

Step 5: Check again—Re-examine

Once you have established a reliable baseline, asked Guilt Questions about the suspected activity, and observed a cluster of clues, it's time to move into the Re-examination phase. The purpose of this phase is to validate your observations of the "clue cluster." To do this, you need to ask some more Control Questions, and then ask the same Guilt Question, or one very similar to the one that initiated the clue cluster that you observed. This is best done by rephrasing the initial Guilt Question and raising it again as naturally as possible. When you ask the rephrased question, once again look for the deceit clues that were previously in stark contrast to the responses to your Control Questions. What you are looking for at this point is a replication of the same or similar response to a very similar question. For example, in response to your initial Guilt Question, you observed that the person immediately avoided your gaze and changed his or her tone of voice. When you ask the rephrased question, pay close attention to the gaze and tone of voice of the subject to see if it changes again. If it does, it's highly likely that person is lying. You may also want to observe some additional lying signs for further confirmation, such as micro-expressions and text-bridging (explained in more detail on pages 84 and 111).

Scenario: After your Control Questions, you asked the salesman the question, "Is this the best deal you can give me on this car?" and he increased his blinking and rubbed his nose as he responded with, "Yes that's the lowest deal I can offer you." Then you proceed to talk in more general terms in relation to the car, asking more questions. These may be control-type questions that the salesman will answer truthfully. For example, you ask the salesman, "Does this model come with a sunroof?" and, "What is the fuel consumption?" while you observe the rate of his blinking and the frequency of his rubbing his nose. After a few more general questions you ask the Guilt Question, "So is the best deal you can offer me, $35,000? I thought you might be able to do better than that." If the salesman again rubs his nose and his blink rate increases—he is most likely lying. Your next step may be to suggest to him that you will visit another dealership or that you would like to see if he could talk to his manager and see if a better deal can be struck—because you know it can!

Re-examination is a good safety measure for you to ensure that the clue cluster you initially observed is replicated in response to the rephrased question. This will increase accuracy and minimize the chance of a coincidental response. For example, it may have been the case (in the scenario) that when asked the Guilt Question, the salesman rubbed his nose because it was itchy, and at the same time he had a small particle or eyelash irritating his eye.

By re-examining and observing the same behavioral response on two occasions, both in stark contrast to the responses to your Control Questions, you are able to validate your suspicions. Equally important is that you are able to discount your suspicions if you don't see a replication of the same response—the person could be telling the truth. Remaining objective and approaching each individual with an open mind as to whether the person is guilty or not will help you discern lies from the truth.

With practice, you should be able to carry out this five-step process a number of times as part of the same conversation. You can repeat the process as many times as you feel is necessary to validate your suspicion, or equally as important, to discount it.

MAGIC in Action

Step 1. Motivation: Does the person have a motivation to lie? Some salespeople are very motivated to lie, as they work on a sales commission or sales performance based salary.

Step 2. Ask Control Questions (ones the person will answer truthfully) and observe eye contact, hand movements, blink rate, tone of voice, and body movements to establish a behavioral baseline.

Customer asks, "Are these on sale?" or, "Do these come with preloaded applications?" The customer already knows the answers and is observing the verbal and nonverbal signs associated with the salesperson's truthful answers.

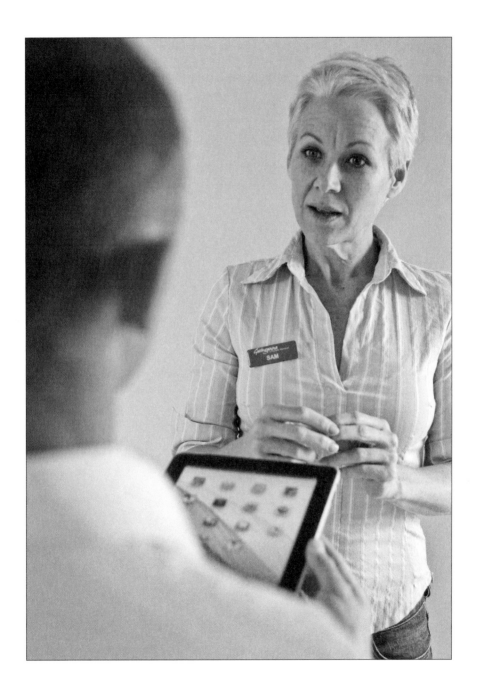

Steps 3 & 4 conducted simultaneously. Guilt Questions: Ask Guilt Questions in order to provide the opportunity for the person to tell the truth or to lie—it's his or her choice.

Indicators: Are there clusters of lying indicators in response to the Guilt Question?

Guilt Question: Customer asks "Do other stores near here stock this brand?" The salesperson answers, "Does anyone else sell these—no, we are definitely the only store around here that sells them, definitely."

Indicators: The customer observes a change from the behavioral baseline. A clue cluster appears as the salesperson answers untruthfully: The question is repeated, the mouth is subtly covered, the body posture becomes closed, eye contact is broken momentarily, and the answer is overemphasized.

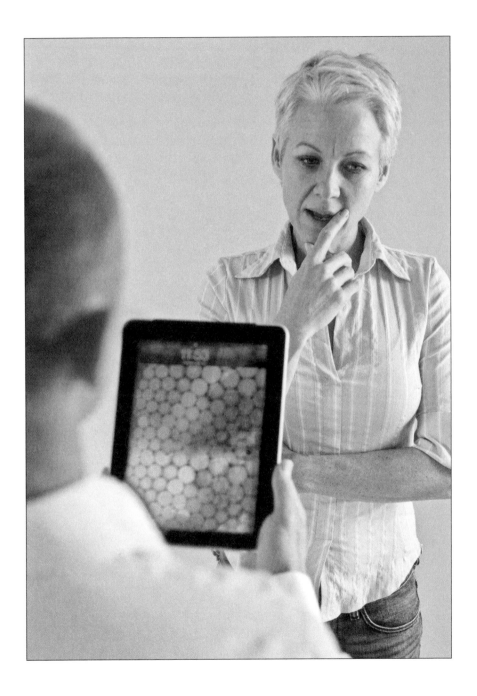

Step 5 (two parts). Check Again: Re-examine using Control Questions followed by Guilt Questions, and observe if the clue cluster returns.

Customer asks Control Questions, "Can it connect to the Internet using wireless?" and, "Is it possible to play games on this?" The salesperson answers truthfully and the behavioral baseline returns—clue cluster is absent.

Customer asks a Guilt Question, "Is this the best price you can sell it to me for?" The salesperson answers, "Well, uh, yes, and it's a great deal. I have never seen it sold any cheaper, anywhere." As the salesperson answers, the clue cluster returns—the nose is touched, partially covering the mouth, closed body posture is repeated, eye contact is again broken, and speech doesn't flow smoothly and is overemphasized.

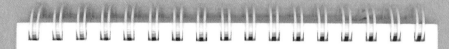

Summary of Main Points:

The MAGIC Lie Detection Model is an easy-to-remember process that may be applied to all situations. You may find it helpful to use this summary to refresh your memory. If you would like more detailed information, I suggest you read the entire section titled *Lie-Detection Process—It's MAGIC!*

Motivation: Does the person have a motivation to lie? Motivations include: to protect from embarrassment; to make a positive impression; to gain an advantage; and to avoid punishment. You'll be more accurate if you remain objective, so don't assume the person is lying—be aware that the person may have the motivation to lie, but is actually telling the truth.

Ask Control Questions, to establish a baseline: When you initially turn on your "Liedar," observe the verbal and nonverbal responses to Control Questions— ones the person will answer truthfully. This will give you a behavioral baseline. Take your time doing this, as it will create a reliable platform to then detect changes in behavior if the person lies.

Guilt Questions: To identify a liar you need to first provide the opportunity to lie. For this to occur, you must ask a Guilt Question or two—subtly. This is best done as part of a normal conversation, as it denies the opportunity for the person to hide deceit clues from you.

Indicators: Are there lying indicators that stand out to you, from the baseline behavior you observed when asking the Control Questions? Did they occur in a clue cluster and in quick succession? When this occurs in response to a guilt question, your "Liedar" should activate. Some deceit clues are listed at the end of this section.

Check Again: Re-examine. To do this, repeat stages MAGI (above) and validate your previous observations of the clue cluster. If you observe a similar clue cluster to a previous Guilt Question, it's likely you've caught yourself a liar.

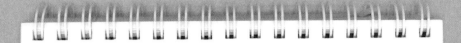

Some Deceit Clues: Finger, hand, leg, and foot movement, or absence of movement; speech pattern changes, increased mispronunciation, throat clearing, exaggerated swallowing, or stuttering; inconsistent eye movement (fabricating not recalling); less eye contact or vastly increased eye contact; itchy nose; closed body posture, leaning back or placing arms across the body to create a barrier; hands in front of mouth or eyes; extended blink followed by a hand to the face; contradictions between "what is said" and "what is gestured" (nodding "yes" but saying "no"); feigning tiredness, (e.g. fake yawning); increased embellishment and overly detailed answers; and conflicting micro-expressions.

LYING SIGNS

There are many individual deceit clues or lying signs a person may exhibit when lying. In this section, we'll cover the majority of known and proven behavioral indicators of lying. This will get you focused on the right areas and get you started quickly. However, you shouldn't feel limited to the deceit clues in this book. If you follow the five-step MAGIC Model we looked at in the previous section, you may discover other indicators that specifically apply to a particular person. Remember, it's a change in behavior you are looking for between the Control Questions and the Guilt Questions. For example, I know a person who usually carries her glasses with her, putting them on periodically. After establishing a behavioral baseline, on each occasion I ask her a Guilt Question. She puts her glasses on as she answers. The most likely reason she does this is that she is attempting to place a barrier between her eyes and mine in an effort to hide her guilty eyes. I've not seen any academic research that supports this particular behavior as a lying sign. However, by following the five step MAGIC Model and having an understanding of counter-measures that liars may use, I have found a very reliable deceit clue that applies to this person in particular.

To ensure the accuracy of your initial attempts at lie detection, I suggest you focus primarily on the lying signs discussed below. However, as you become more accustomed to the MAGIC Lie Detection Model process and more observant of changes in behavior, you can widen your focus and see if you can identify lying signs specific to particular people.

When you begin putting your newfound knowledge into practice, you will notice some people are more susceptible to "leaking" a particular type of deceit clue. If you don't allow deceivers the knowledge that you can identify when they are lying (preventing them the opportunity to hide behind a counter-measure) they will continue to exhibit these lying signs, making it very easy to identify their deceit on future occasions. The person I mentioned before still puts her glasses on whenever she lies. In fact, I won't ask Guilt Questions of this person unless I know she has her glasses with her. Of course, this lying sign has an expiration date—when she needs to wear glasses constantly!

Most people do exhibit some sort of sign when they lie. As we discussed earlier, the signs of lying become more obvious when there is a large cognitive load or when there is a lot of emotion attached to the lie (such as significant consequences if they're caught, triggering feelings of guilt, anxiety, or excitement). When a lie is told, if further questioned, the liar will need to create more lies in support of lies told previously. This increases his or her emotional level, which can lead to an increase in the amount of lying signs that are leaked. This occurs with almost everyone, but not all. This doesn't apply to pathological liars, liars who lie continuously, often believing their lies, which are usually exaggerations used to make an impression or gain an advantage. For example, a pathological liar may tell people that Mick Jagger has been a close friend for years, or that President Obama lived on the same street or went to the same school as the liar, if it allows the liar to manipulate how he or she is positioned within a social or professional group. Dangerously, pathological liars believe these lies and have difficulty distinguishing between fact and fiction, making it difficult to identify their lying signs as the emotional component, as it is either mitigated or absent altogether.

Pathological liars feel little or no emotion when they lie, and they lie constantly. This makes them particularly tricky customers, as it's almost impossible to establish a reliable behavioral baseline because they lie so often, causing the baseline itself to be based on lies. Additionally, due to the lack of emotion when lying, they don't demonstrate the usual lying signs, and as they don't lie with any particular motive, it is difficult to differentiate between when the lies told are immaterial and trivial, and when the lie is a significant one. Fortunately there aren't many pathological liars in society. However, if you do encounter one (and it will be obvious to you), I still recommend adopting the five-step MAGIC Model.

Perhaps the best way to deal with a pathological liars is to structure your questions such that they can only answer "yes" or "no." This way the truth will be the answer they don't give!

Another tricky kind of customer is one who has told the same lie on many previous occasions—the rehearsed liar. As this kind of liar has practiced and rehearsed the material on several occasions, the response appears more fluid. This is because there isn't a heavy cognitive load on the mind (because the person is not fabricating while speaking), and there is also less emotion attached to the lie (as the person has told the lie many times and has been desensitized). Interestingly, studies have shown that rehearsed lies sound more convincing, but when they are told, the person displays more nonverbal signs of deception. While rehearsed liars may sound more convincing, to the lie detector they look guiltier.[20]

This section will provide you with some great deceit clues to identify when a person is lying, and I encourage you to practice these techniques as often as possible. Challenging family members to try to lie to you can be good fun. Importantly, this also can provide you with accurate feedback when you get it wrong—don't worry, they'll let you know. When you do make a mistake, review what made you think it was a lie and learn from it; this will make you harder to beat next time. Also, challenge them again following the MAGIC Model and look for different deceit clues.

When you identify a reliable deceit clue of a family member, try not to let that person know what the sign is. Until the family member can pick up what the clue is, it won't be possible to hide it from you, and lying to you successfully will be impossible. How frustrating for your family member—enjoy it!

While I don't prioritize a particular lying sign above others, I do believe the focus of the astute lie detector should be on areas that individuals are unaware of or over which they have little control. While highly conductive channelled responses such as finger movement and eye contact cannot be discounted, it is the mannerisms liars don't expect you to be watching or over which they have little control that can provide you a greater insight, such as micro-expressions, text-bridging, and lower limb movement. In the following sections we'll cover all the areas that will provide you the best information for accurately detecting lying signs.

It's Written All Over the Face

The Eyes

The eyes are an incredibly valuable source of information that humans naturally rely upon to assess other people's personality and emotional states. This is particularly evident when we look at photographs, as we cannot rely upon body movement and speech. When shown a photograph of a person, the first place we look is the eyes in an effort to assess the emotion of that person. Try this yourself—look at a photo of a stranger and see where you look first. On almost every occasion it will be the eyes. We have a natural thirst to obtain information from the eyes. Without access to the eyes (for example when a person wears sunglasses) we are inhibited in our assessment of other people. Would you feel comfortable making a major purchase from a salesman, or forming a trusting relationship with a person, who wore sunglasses all the time, and you never once were able to see the person's eyes?

This book reveals a number of the lying signs or deceit clues individuals may exhibit when attempting to deceive you. My favorite and most successful area to focus upon to identify if a person is lying is the eyes. It appears very difficult for people to fabricate information or invent a story and maintain normal eye behavior. For example, you may ask a person to answer a question very quickly. This usually results in the person's eyes moving quickly from side to side and looking downwards slightly while attempting to get the brain in order to respond. Similarly, a person's eyes may stall or freeze in a particular position as the person attempts to respond to a question. It's as if our brain and our eyes are hardwired together, and when the brain is put under pressure, the eyes reveal it. The three key areas of the eyes to focus on are eye contact, blink rate, and eye movement, which are discussed below. When you start practicing your lie-detection skills, I suggest you commence with the eyes.

Eye Contact: Eyes are said to be the window to the soul. They can also present a window of opportunity for the astute Human Lie Detector, but not solely by the method most commonly thought of—eye contact.

Most people, when asked how they identify a liar, will state they observe the person's eyes and see if the person can maintain regular eye contact. As previously mentioned, eyes are controlled by a highly conductive channel that provides a lot of feedback to the brain. This allows liars a degree of control, and they can therefore manipulate the amount of eye contact given to the person questioning them to assist with disguising their guilt. Often liars will deliberately increase the amount of eye contact in the hope of appearing more sincere. However, via your Control Questions, you should be able to ascertain what the normal amount of eye contact is for any particular person. Sometimes it can be very obvious in situations where the person has a certain amount of eye contact in response to Control Questions, and as soon as Guilt Questions are asked, the person increases eye contact noticeably. Again, what you are looking for is an increase in eye contact or a decrease in eye contact in response to Guilt Questions. The amount of eye contact can be manipulated, but it is difficult for a person transitioning from telling the truth to lying to maintain consistency. So look for inconsistency.

HANDY HINT: Children and inexperienced liars, or ones that are surprised by your question, will immediately maintain less eye contact with you. They will instantaneously look away, may raise their hand in front of their eyes to break contact, or may pretend to be distracted by something and look away or rub their eyes. When they have composed themselves, they will bounce back to having normal eye contact. It's this initial break in eye contact that is a great clue for you to look for.

Blink Rate: Our normal rate of blinking during conversation is about twenty-six times per minute, though this can increase significantly during periods of stress.[21] Regardless of whether a person is stressed or not, if you observe a significant change in his or her blink rate (slower or faster) when you switch from asking Control Questions to Guilt Questions, you can assume the person is lying. A person may blink slower when answering Guilt Questions for one of two reasons: first, the person wants to break eye contact, but doesn't want to turn away, as that would be an obvious sign of guilt; second, the person's mind is consuming a lot of energy fabricating a response (cognitive overload—close to mental bankruptcy), and this causes the person to have an extended blink time. Similarly, liars may increase their blink rate or flutter their eyes when lying, behaviors which are also signs of wanting to minimize the amount of eye contact. The deceit motivation for liars subconsciously changing their blink rate isn't something we need to concentrate on, as our focus is simply to observe a change in the rate between Control Questions and Guilt Questions.

A word of warning: People may extend their blink time, blink frequently (fluttering their eyes), or break eye contact simply because they don't wish to answer the question. This reticence could simply be because they are uncomfortable with the information you're asking for and would like to block it out. People will also increase their blink rate when they are thinking hard about something. This something may be the truth. So a change in blink rate by itself is not a reliable sign of deceit; it needs to be taken into account with other lying signs.

HANDY HINT: If there is an extended blink followed by a hand movement to the face, this is a fair indicator the person may be lying. These movements can indicate the person subconsciously wants to block out your presence by forming a barrier (the hand) and is also attempting to block you out (visually) by extending the blink time.

Eye Movement: Another very interesting sign to observe is the movement of the eyes themselves. With some individuals (but not all) this can tell you very quickly if they are remembering or creating/fabricating. This technique is based on Neuro Linguistic Programming (NLP), which was initiated by the work of John Grinder and Richard Bandler at the University of California in the 1970s.[22] NLP is an entire subject in its own right, and there are many companies that offer training in this subject if you want to pursue it. Rather than bombard you with pages of academic theory on NLP, I think it's best to just give you the critical information that relates directly to lie detection.

When you experiment with this technique, you'll notice it works very well with some people and not at all with others. As such, it should be used in addition to other lying signs before determining if a person is lying. I highly recommend after you read this section that you have a go at it. Try it out on a friend or family member, even a child. Have some fun with it.

The basic premise of how this works is that the eyes move in particular directions depending upon what the mind is doing. People are hardwired into this practice, and it's very difficult to change or manipulate consistently in an attempt to try to disguise what is being thought. People are quite capable of disguising the movement of their eyes when they are conscious of doing so. However, this is not natural, nor is it possible to maintain such a high degree of control consistently. That's one of the reasons it's a worthwhile area to look for deceit clues.

NOTE: NLP has been criticized and discounted by some and highly acclaimed and supported by others. I have found the technique to work very effectively with some people and not at all with others. Regardless, having some knowledge of NLP provides you with another weapon in your lie-detection arsenal.

As I am writing this book for you, all the directions of left and right are given from your position as you are observing the person. If I say the person will look right, that means your right (their left). Because some of the eye movements you will be attempting to observe can be very rapid, it's important that you instinctively know which direction means what. As such, I have created a model specifically for lie detection purposes.

When asked a question, right-handed individuals' eyes should:

- Move either horizontally or diagonally upwards—right (your right), if they are remembering something that actually happened. This indicates to you they have actually experienced what they are telling you in response to your question; or,

- Move either horizontally or diagonally upwards—left (your left), if they are creating something in their own mind, something they have not seen or heard before. This indicates to you the person has not seen or heard what the person is telling you about in response to your question. The person is creating/fabricating.

NOTE: The direction of eye movement for a left-handed person will be the opposite of the above.

Because you will be attempting to assess a number of lying signs simultaneously, for simplicity it's best to just concentrate on the upper 180° movements of the eyes. The lower 180° movements also demonstrate cognitive activity, though they are not as pertinent to lie detection. Because eye movement can be very rapid, particularly when people are recalling or creating a very quick response such as "yes" or "no," it's best if you can ask a question that requires them to talk for some time. This will increase the amount of time the eyes will track back and forth or remain in a particular position, allowing you more time to assess whether the person is creating/fabricating or recalling an actual event. Also, when people are answering "yes" or "no," they may naturally blink, which will hide the direction of the eyes, or deliberately blink for an extended period of time before responding. Either way, you will have lost the opportunity to assess the reaction. So try to come up with a question that will require a response using a number of words or sentences if possible.

Try this: Ask a child or family member (preferably a child, as the signs are more obvious) to sit down opposite you. Sit so you can observe the eyes clearly and ask the person to describe truthfully in as much detail as possible a place or event that you have both been to (so they tell you the truth). Have the person talk about it in detail for a while. Observe the direction of the eyes, but don't tell the person what you are looking for, or the person will be able to disguise it. Then ask the person to make up a fake story about an event that occurred at a place where the person has not been. You want the person to fabricate/create images. For example, the person could tell you about camping in Africa and riding on a wild elephant. Have the person expand on the answer in detail. Ask them to describe what the camping area looked like, what other animals were there, did the person feed them, what did the elephant look like in real life, what were the trees like, and what color the tent was. Ask the person to make up a story about what was done on that camping trip. As the person expands on this fictitious story, you should notice the eyes tracking in a different direction to when the person was telling the truth. If you do, this is NLP in practice.

HANDY HINT: If the person looks right, it is right (correct/truthful). Right = Right. If the person looks left, it is a lie (created/fabricated). Left = Lie.

Rule Exceptions:

1. Sometimes a person will look straight ahead with little or no eye movement with the eyes appearing to be unfocused. This is also a sign that the person is recalling an actual event.

2. As with all lying signs, some will manifest quite profoundly with some people and not at all with others, so you may find this technique doesn't work with all people. This is one of the reasons this book provides so many different clues to look for when a person is lying. If one particular technique doesn't work on a person, you can rely on several others and still improve your accuracy.

While I have attempted to make this a very simple rule to follow, as with all human behavior, there are no fixed rules. The above rule indicates the responses for a right-handed/right-orientated person. A left-handed/orientated person will have the exact opposite eye movement in response to questions. There is also a very small minority of right-handed people whose eyes will react as would a left-handed person. All this might sound very confusing, but it doesn't have to be.

All you need to do is identify the orientation of the person during your Control Questioning. Simply ask the person about an event that you know he or she has experienced and observe the direction of the eyes. You may ask a number of questions to confirm the orientation. Then when you ask the Guilt Question, if you observe the eyes moving in the opposite direction from when the Control Questions were asked, it is likely the person is fabricating their response.

Remember, it's not the eye movement alone that will indicate the person has lied. It's eye movement that indicates the person is creating/fabricating something together with other lying signs, forming a clue cluster that indicates deception. When looking for eye movement, remember it can be extremely rapid so you need to be very observant.

Okay, let's put this into practice—time for some fun!

Step 1. Select a family member or friend as your victim. Ask the person some questions about the events or experiences you know he or she has been through and observe the movement of the eyes. This allows you to observe the orientation. If right-handed, the person will most likely be looking across to the (your) right or upwards to the (your) right when recalling what you have asked.

Step 2. Then ask the person to tell you four things he or she did last weekend, but make one of them a lie. As they are doing this, observe the eye movement. The answer with the *different* eye movement is the lie because the person has fabricated this answer, and the eyes tracked differently.

NOTE: Remember, sometimes people will look straight ahead with little or no eye movement when recalling real events, and if they do this naturally, this drill won't work. However, if your victim is not one of these people (based on your Control Questions) and tries to be particularly difficult by just staring directly at you in the hope that this will throw you off the scent, then pay particular attention to any change in his or her blink rate and/or speech pattern. If there is a pause just before one of the answers or one of the answers is given more slowly or delivered more quickly than the other three—that's the lie.

HANDY HINT: Liars may look away very briefly as they tell a lie to break eye contact; however, they may also disguise their guilt by looking back very quickly. The break in eye contact is a giveaway of guilt, and they look back searching for feedback from you on whether or not they got away with the lie. At this point, remain stony-faced (don't give away any clues) and pause the conversation. This is very difficult for liars to deal with, as they don't receive any feedback from you, either verbal or facial, as to whether or not they got away with the lie. Often this causes them to start talking, and it is this that will really expose them. The speech will be rapid, overly detailed, and/or illogical or their eyes will dart back and forth as they assess the situation and replay their answer in their head, making their own assessment on whether they got away with the lie or not. Liars hate silence!

Earlier in the book I mentioned that a person's pupils might dilate when lying. This can be another useful indicator, but unless you have a visual recording of the person, such as a police interview tape or media interview of high quality, it's very difficult to monitor and assess. Additionally there are some very small movements around the eyes that can be indicators of deception, which will be covered under the section titled *Micro-expressions* on page 84. However, in respect to the eyes, the three primary areas that you will find most useful to monitor are eye contact, blink rate, and eye movement.

Often liars will deliberately increase the amount of eye contact in the hope of appearing more sincere.

Liars may look away immediately after having lied.

Liars may raise their hand in front of their eyes.

Liars may pretend to be distracted by rubbing their eyes and looking away.

After breaking initial contact, they may look back for feedback to see if the lie has been accepted.

Creating or fabricating something. Looks to the left.

Recalling a real event. Looks to the right.

The Nose Knows

If you are ever attempting to check the truthfulness of a small, carved, wooden boy called Pinocchio, then I suggest you observe the length of his nose as you ask the Guilt Questions. Unfortunately, human noses don't increase or decrease in size when telling lies, but they can still assist you with detecting deception.

As a matter of course, people will touch their nose from time to time—this is normal. However, some liars will touch their nose with increased frequency. During your Control Questions, observe how often the person touches his or her nose—perhaps not at all. When you ask your Guilt Questions, if the person commences touching the nose, then I recommend undertaking a re-examination, as this could be a lying sign. If this occurs a second time during the re-examination phase, it is unlikely it was a coincidence and more likely a lie.

Liars touch their nose either as a method of momentarily covering their mouth with their hand (giving them a comfort/protection barrier) or because the tissues within their nose become engorged with blood, causing an itching sensation.[23] The liar then necessarily touches the nose to alleviate this itchy feeling. Doctor Charles Wolf (University of Utah) and Doctor Alan Hirsch (Smell and Taste Treatment and Research Foundation, Chicago) reviewed in detail the testimony by former president Bill Clinton in relation to the Monica Lewinsky matter.[24] In addition to other lying signs that Clinton exhibited during his testimony, Doctors Hirsch and Wolf found when the former president was telling the truth, he barely touched his nose at all. However, when he made statements which were less than truthful, he touched his nose regularly.[25]

If you have the time, it's a worthwhile exercise doing Internet video searches on people who have been interviewed by police or media after which they have proven to be lying. While you don't have the opportunity to ask Control Questions, you may notice these people touching their nose frequently. On its own, nose touching isn't proof positive of deception, but when it occurs in the re-examination phase together with other lying signs, your "Liedar" is accurate.

Liars touch their nose more frequently—partially to cover the mouth and also due to increased blood flow to the nose, causing an itchy feeling.

The Mouth

As a child, my father used to say to me, "David, I can always tell when you're lying—your mouth is moving and words are coming out!" Gee, thanks, Dad. Regardless of how truthful the statement was, he was correct about one thing— the mouth can be observed to detect lies. This section will look at lying signs *of the mouth* rather than what is actually said *by the mouth*. Verbal signs of lying will be covered later under the section *Speaking with forked tongue* on page 108.

There are two common tactics used by people who are lying—they either attempt to hide their mouth or hold their mouth closed. It's as if the liar subconsciously wants to hide the source of the lie itself. You may have noticed particularly with young children, who have yet to learn how to hide their deceit effectively, that when they tell a lie or inadvertently say something that they wished they hadn't, they instantaneously put their hand across their mouth. This is sometimes a very overt and animated gesture. The same principle applies to adults; however, the signs have become more subtle as they have learned self-control and also to minimize the signs of lying. Adult liars may attempt to hide their mouth as they lie by turning away slightly, holding a pen to their mouth as they speak, or, as mentioned in the previous section, they may cover their mouth with their hand as they touch their nose.

The next time you are with a group of people or attend a meeting where a discussion is taking place, see if you can spot a person who has fingers or a singular finger across the lips. Sometimes you may observe people actually pinching their lips together with their fingers or resting a thumb under the chin while the index finger rests across their lips. The person who is doing this in the group would like to say something but is holding back, either through courtesy (waiting for a turn to speak) or because the person disagrees with what is being said and is holding back from saying so. The same holds true for some liars; they'll pinch their lip or put their fingers across their lips in what appears to be a subconscious attempt to stop the truth from slipping out.

Another way the mouth can be complicit in deception is by manufacturing a false smile. I'm sure there have been occasions where you have observed a smile, and you can sense it's not genuine. The most obvious way of identifying a genuine smile from an insincere one is that a fake smile primarily only affects the lower half of the face, predominantly with the mouth alone, while eyes don't really get involved. Take the opportunity to look in the mirror and manufacture a smile using the lower half your face only. When you do this, assess how happy your face really looks—is it genuine? A genuine smile will have an impact on the muscles and wrinkles around the eyes, and, more subtly, the skin between the eyebrow and upper eyelid is lowered slightly with true enjoyment. The genuine smile can affect the entire face. It's as if when there is true happiness to be had, the whole face wants to join the party, crow's feet and all!

A genuine smile is also formed more slowly on the face than a manufactured smile and is always symmetrical. There's a pleasant emotional build-up that creates a real smile, and this takes time. A manufactured smile doesn't have the real emotion attached to it and is simply a decision to make certain muscles act in a particular way, which happens much faster than with a genuine smile. For the same reason, a genuine smile fades more slowly from the face—it doesn't simply switch off like a manufactured smile.

HANDY HINT: If you want to know if you have really amused a person, in addition to watching for muscle movement around the eyes, watch how slowly the smile leaves the person's face. Having a genuine smile is like having an old friend over for dinner: You don't want them to leave quickly, and similarly, the genuine smile departs slowly. Having a fake smile is like saying goodbye to a pushy door-to-door salesman: You can't shut the door quickly enough!

The fact that a person manufactures a smile doesn't necessarily mean the person is lying. People that do this may be smiling to cover up the fact that they are unhappy, want to appear pleasant to you, or are simply being polite. However, if the smile comes from the mouth alone, it's not genuine. Statistically, liars smile less often than truthful people.[26] However, as you are aware, liars will also deliberately manufacture a smile as a counter-measure to indicate friendliness or that they are comfortable and relaxed about your questions. For this reason it is important for you to be able to distinguish between a genuine and a fake smile.

HANDY HINT: A great way to practice distinguishing between real and false smiles is by watching movies. Observe actors' faces when they are smiling or laughing, particularly around the eyes. I find this very interesting, as you can quite quickly notice whether the actor is actually laughing or is acting (smiling with only the mouth). Sometimes in a scene when two actors are laughing together, they really are laughing.

Another way the mouth may attempt to lie to you is by creating a deliberate yawn. If you are talking at length with a person who is lying, sometimes this person will yawn. This is most likely a counter-strategy to try to convince you they are not feeling any stress. Again, if you notice that a person starts to yawn (usually combined with the body leaning back and arms and/or legs spreading out widely) when you're asking your Guilt Questions, return to some Control Questions and see if the yawning stops. If so, proceed to the re-examination phase.

Other possible signs of deceit from the mouth include dry lips, lips with less color, or very tense, pursed lips—held together by muscles rather than using the hands to stop the truth slipping out. These can also be signs of stress unrelated to deception but are another clue to look out for.

Scenario: I recently watched an in-depth and extended interview with a famous sportsman. He was seated on a sofa with his wife and was being asked a whole range of questions. This allowed me to observe his behavioral baseline.

The interviewer asked, "You two have been married for some time, you seem happy, but it must be hard being separated so often?" The sportsman answered, "Yes, we are happy, and it is hard, but I'm committed to my sport." The sportsman's body language and all other signs remained consistent with that of the previous part of the interview. However, the interviewer then asked, "So there is no girl chasing or affairs going on, like Tiger Woods did?" Immediately and for the first time, the sportsman adjusted his seating position, turned his head away from the interviewer, and rubbed his nose as he answered, "No, nothing like that." For legal reasons I can't name the person; however, I'm confident that in response to that question, he lied. There was an obvious clue cluster in response to that question and that question alone throughout the interview. He was lying.

Fake smile: The mouth can be complicit in deception by manufacturing a false smile. The fake smile is a polite smile.

Real smile: In the real smile the muscles around the eyes are triggered, and the whole face joins in. If you cover the lower half of both photos just under the nose and observe the eyes, it becomes obvious which is the real smile and which is fake.

Liars may hold their mouth closed or pinch their lips.

Liars may attempt to hide their mouth with their hands or by turning their body slightly away.

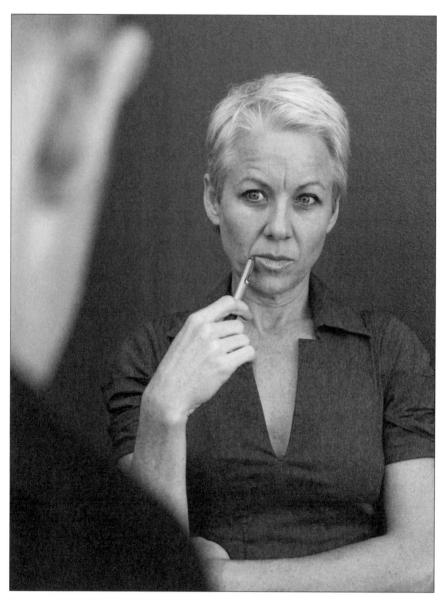

Liars may attempt to cover their mouth with an item, such as a pen.

Micro-Expressions—Flashes of Falsehood

Identification and interpretation of micro-expressions were significantly advanced by the work of Professor Ekman, a pioneer in this subject area. The popular television show *Lie to Me* dramatized some of the pioneering work of Professor Ekman, who is loosely represented as Dr. Cal Lightman (played by Tim Roth) in the series. The topic itself is a subject in its own right and requires in-depth study of many academic journals, articles, and research results to have a comprehensive understanding—but you don't need to endure this, as I've done all the hard work for you! However, if you want to learn more about this particular aspect of lie detection, I recommend undertaking the online training offered by Professor Ekman's group.[27]

The nature of this book is not to provide an in-depth academic understanding on all facets of lie detection, just the crucial segments of information that will quickly lead the reader on the path to becoming a more effective lie detector. Micro-expressions form an essential part of this.

As we discussed earlier in the book, when people lie, they feel a certain amount of emotion (Emotional Response), which can vary from stress, guilt, and anxiety to a certain feeling of exhilaration. These emotions can lead to certain physiological changes (Sympathetic Nervous Response), which can result in certain guilty symptoms, such as fidgeting and avoiding eye contact, etc. Earlier in the book we also discussed the fact that liars will deliberately instigate counter-measures to hide the symptoms of their guilt (Cognitive Response). We also discovered that some symptoms were easy for the liar to disguise and control (e.g. hand movement and eye contact) and others were not (blink rate and eye movement). Micro-expressions are expressions of emotion displayed on the face of a person. They appear extremely briefly (as quickly as 1/25 of a second) and are usually missed by the casual observer. These micro-expressions are so instantaneous that the person expressing them has no control over them. Therefore, a liar cannot instigate a counter-measure in an effort to mask these emotions from you. Micro-expressions display the true inner emotion of a person before there is time to hide it. This makes micro-expressions a fantastic tool for the Human Lie Detector.

Another reason why they are so useful is that regardless of culture, race, or upbringing, the micro-expressions of happiness, sadness, disgust, contempt, anger, surprise, and fear are universal and don't change, so they can be applied to all people.[28]

When a lie detector observes the face, it's important to remember that it can do a lot of things that are independent of emotion, for example make gestures. Facial gestures such as a wink are culturally specific and cannot be applied across all people. Additionally, people develop and use certain facial mannerisms that are designed to communicate information to another person, such as a raised eyebrow. The easiest way to distinguish between a facial gesture or mannerism and a micro-expression is that micro-expressions appear as a "flash" or "twitch" on the person's face. Contrarily, facial gestures and mannerisms are slower and more obvious, as they are designed to communicate information to another person. Micro-expressions are involuntary flashes of emotions on the face.

The primary thing to look for when observing micro-expressions is a disparity between the micro-expressed emotion and what is actually said. For example, a person may be asked a question, "I was told that Simon was fired yesterday—what do you think of that?" In response to this, the person (for the briefest period) shows a slight smile (wrinkling around the eyes, not just the mouth), but responds, "That's a real shame, he was a nice guy." The incongruity between the micro-expressed happiness and the statement expressing sadness or loss is obvious. The person's micro-expression betrayed the fact that he was happy that Simon was no longer in the workplace.

If you're like most people, you have never noticed micro-expressions before. You have to be fast to catch these tricky little expressions, but they do exist. With practice, you'll be surprised how regularly you start to notice them. They may appear to you as a twitch or just a flicker on the person's face. When you do notice one, it's important to then listen to what is simultaneously said and see if it conflicts with the micro-expressed emotion. If it doesn't conflict, the person is stating what is truly felt. If it does conflict, the person is hiding true emotions from you.

EXAMPLE: Micro-expressions reveal how a person "really" feels; they cannot be masked from you. A person may say to you, while smiling politely, "Oh, that's fine, I'm happy to meet John at Shakimra's café," but as this is said, you notice the person's upper lip is raised and lowered very quickly and the eyebrows flicker downwards. This is the micro-expression of disgust. While the person is deliberately showing you happiness/politeness, there is an inner emotion of disgust in regards to the meeting. The person is masking feelings of disgust about a particular aspect of what has been proposed.

I don't believe it is necessary to study the many muscle groups and technical aspects surrounding the facial movement for each emotion. These facial emotions are consistent across all races and cultures, and you should be able to recognize them when you see them. However, I have provided some examples of the seven micro-expressions below. This will assist you in recognizing them more instantaneously.

Because micro-expressions occur so very quickly and are easy to miss, each of the following examples recommends you focus on one particular area. Each area is most likely to give you an indication of that emotion, rather than focusing on all areas for that micro-expression. This doesn't mean the other areas can be discounted, but I suggest you focus your attention on the recommended area until you become more practiced at instantaneously recognizing the seven emotions.

NOTE: The primary thing you really need to practice is capturing the micro-expression itself. Then ask yourself, did that emotion conflict with what the person said?

Micro-expressions are involuntary flashes of emotion on the face. Look for mismatches between what is said and micro-expressions.

Happiness: The person smiles symmetrically. The cheeks are raised and there is real movement around the eyes. The skin between the eyebrow and upper eyelid is lowered slightly—but this is hard to spot, so focus your attention around the eyes. Was there movement? If the eyes aren't really smiling, it's a fake.

Sadness: The corners of the lips are pulled down, and the inner edges of the eyebrows are slightly raised. Focus your attention on the edges of the mouth—were they pulled downwards?

Anger: The lips become thinner and are pressed together or tense and opened slightly. The inner edges of the eyebrows are lowered toward the bridge of the nose, causing a furrow between the eyebrows. The upper eyelids are raised, opening the eyes, and the person will glare; the eyes remain wide open. Focus your attention on either micro-expression—the mouth or the eyes.

Contempt: One side of the mouth is tightened and pulled back. This may just look like a twitch or a flicker. It may be combined with the person tilting the head backwards slightly. This is the only emotion that is displayed with an "asymmetrical" response. Focus your attention on the mouth—if the movement wasn't symmetrical, you just saw contempt.

Disgust: The upper lip remains full and is relaxed as it is raised symmetrically and may expose the teeth. The nose often becomes wrinkled. Focus attention on the upper lip—was it raised and then lowered very quickly—did it remain relaxed and full?

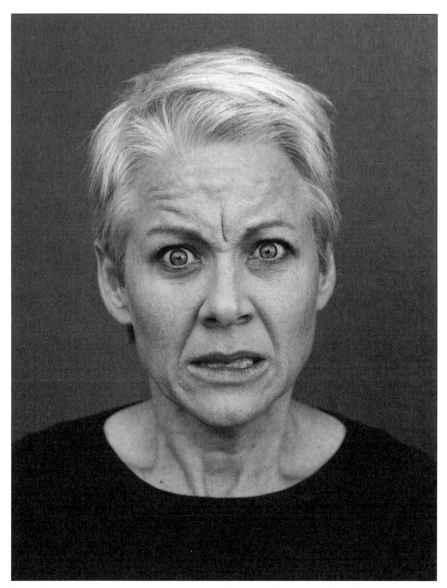

Fear: The eyebrows are raised, but they are flattened (less curved) as they are pushed together. The eyes widen. The mouth is widened horizontally thinning the lips. It will be tempting to focus on the eyes; however, the eyes can appear similar between fear and surprise. Focus on the mouth—was it widened horizontally towards the ears?

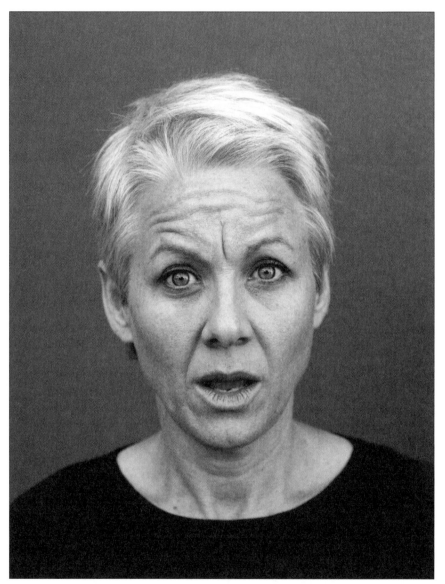

Surprise: The eyes widen and the eyebrows are lifted—but only briefly. The eyebrows remain curved. The mouth opens slightly as the jaw drops—the lips remain relaxed. People faking surprise will open their mouth too wide and leave their eyebrows raised for too long. Focus on the eyebrows—were they raised and lowered very quickly—did they remain curved?

Confusion Between Micro-Expressions

Because of the speed of these tricky flashes of falsehood, some micro-expressions appear similar until you get used to picking up on them. I think the hardest to distinguish are anger from disgust and fear from surprise. Below, I have outlined the primary distinguishing features of these four micro-expressions to assist you with quickly determining the difference between them.

Anger vs. Disgust: Anger can look like disgust, as they both cause the brow to be crunched up and lowered. However, the most discernible differences can be seen around the eyes and the mouth.

Angry Eyes: Glaring and more open; eyebrows are lowered and drawn together.

Disgusted Eyes: The eyes are not as open (as angry eyes), and are often squinted—with eyebrows lowered, not drawn together.

Angry Mouth: The lips are pressed together and become thinner or are opened slightly with tension thinning the lips.

Disgusted Mouth: The upper lip is raised. Both lips remain full and more relaxed—you may see a glimpse of teeth.

Fear vs. Surprise: Fear and Surprise can be confused, as they both cause the eyebrows to be raised and the mouth to open. However, there is a noticeable difference, particularly in respect to the eyebrows and the shape of the mouth.

Fear Eyebrows: Raised but straightened slightly (less curved) and pulled together.

Surprised Eyebrows: Raised but curved.

Fear Mouth: Mouth opens slightly; the lips are pulled back laterally, widening the mouth.

Surprised Mouth: Mouth opens slightly; lips remain full and relaxed.

HANDY HINT: If a person is wearing sunglasses, had plastic surgery, and/or just completed a Botox treatment, forget trying to read that person's face—it will tell you a very confused story!

Scenario: You are at a work function where numerous people are standing around eating and drinking. You suspect Jill, who is right-handed, was with another woman's husband (Brett) on Friday night and not at the football game as she has stated (her alibi). You turn your "Liedar" on.

You spend some time establishing a reliable baseline by asking questions you know the answer to and you know she knows the answer to (e.g., "Jill, remember the office Christmas party last year—what was the name of the restaurant?"). During your Control Questions, you have observed the amount of eye contact she is having with you and her blink rate. You also observed her eyes flash upwards to your right as she recalled what the restaurant looked like. This behavior demonstrates to you NLP (eye tracking) is observable with Jill; she is recalling an actual event—she's telling the truth.

As she previously stated she was at the football match last Friday night, you lead into some Guilt Questions (e.g., "Was it very crowded at the game? How many people do you think were home team fans, based on the colors of the crowd?"). In response to this question you notice two quick blinks (combination of cognitive load and wanting to hide her eyes), and you see her eyes look upwards to the left (creating a picture in her mind, not recalling an actual image) as she responds, "I think there were about an equal number of home supporters and away team supporters." Jill then takes a long drink from her glass as she glances away from you (avoiding eye contact, hiding her mouth with the glass—she may start to have a dry mouth). You look in the direction she glanced toward, and there is nothing of particular interest that would have distracted her. You then have a general conversation (more Control Questions, during which you observe her behavioral baseline). Then you ask her, "Have you heard the rumor around the office that Brett is having an affair?" As soon as you have said this you notice both Jill's eyebrows raise up and down very quickly but remain curved (just a flicker), and her mouth opens just slightly then closes (micro-expression of surprise). She smiles and responds, "Well that's fairly typical for our office.... There's always lots of rumors floating around—nothing surprises me in this place." (There is a total mismatch between her micro-expression of surprise and her statement). As she speaks, she picks up a napkin and wipes her mouth and nose briefly (hiding her mouth and rubbing her itchy nose). She changes the subject (deflection—discussed later in the book on page 112).

What does your "Liedar" say about Jill?

A Body of Lies

Do liars move their bodies more or less when they lie? If you answered "more" or "less" to this question, you answered it correctly. The reason for this is that due to the Sympathetic Nervous Response ("fight or flight" reaction) liars naturally want to move their bodies more, such as adjusting their seating position often, moving their legs, and tapping their fingers. If you asked a person a question and the person did all three of these actions, you would quickly come to the conclusion the person was lying. Liars know this. As highly conductive channels control these movements (ones that provide constant feedback to the brain), they provide a high degree of control to the liar. Therefore, the liar will attempt to control these movements as a counter-strategy (Cognitive Response) to disguise guilt. This can result in liars actually moving their body less frequently than usual as they try to manipulate body movements and hide the urge to move from you. Some liars will move more often and some will move less often. So how are we meant to determine deceit based on body movement?

The answer is actually quite simple. We just need to follow the five steps we covered previously in this section (*Lie-Detection Process*).

Motivation: Does the person have a motivation to lie?

Ask Control Questions: To establish a behavioral baseline.

Guilt Questions: Ask Guilt Questions.

Indicators: Are there lying indicators in clue clusters?

Check Again: Re-examine.

As you are establishing a behavioral baseline, observe how often the person's body moves as you are asking your Control Questions. When you are asking your Guilt Questions, try to identify if there is a sudden increase in body movement or a sudden decrease in body movement; either can indicate deception. If movement increases, the Sympathetic Nervous Response (adrenaline) is causing the person to move more often. Decreased movement indicates that the person is deliberately reducing body movement to disguise guilt.

If you don't notice a difference in the amount of body movement between the Control Questions and the Guilt Questions, this may indicate the person is telling the truth. When observing the body to detect deceit, the best thing to look for is inconsistency in the movements. The below section highlights some of the better body deceit clues to observe when looking for changes in activity between the Control Question and Guilt Question phases. Remember, if the person is lying, there could be either an increase or decrease in movement of these body parts.

Arms and Hands: Sweating palms are often referred to as a sign of a guilty person. In my opinion, it's clearly a sign of stress and may indicate that a person is lying. However, people may be stressed just because they are being challenged on something they said. Additionally, it's impossible to observe when a person starts sweating, stops sweating, and how profusely a person is sweating. For this reason, this indicator cannot be assessed within the five-step lie-detection model (MAGIC) discussed earlier in the book. While it may be beneficial to note that someone has sweaty palms and is therefore stressed, it is not a reliable deceit clue, as it can't be assessed consistently. Therefore, I suggest there are more reliable deceit clues to observe. For example, the person may start to fidget or tap fingers. The fingers may even shake or tremble slightly; these indicators can be assessed within the model. If the deceiver is conscious of the fidgeting, counter-measures may include hands being hidden in pockets, under a desk, or clasped together in an attempt to disguise the fidgeting. The person may even hold on to a chair, pole, or table when speaking to you to minimize arm movement. If you suspect this is occurring, attempt to see how tightly the person is gripping the object; you may notice the grip is tighter than what is normal.

Interestingly, liars rarely steeple their fingers. This is a natural body position often used by people to convey an assurance of strength and confidence. However, liars will sometimes steeple their fingers in front of their face in an effort to form a barrier. Liars often raise their hands to their face, primarily to cover their eyes or mouth or to surreptitiously touch their nose.

HANDY HINT: Remember it is a conflict between what the body says and what is said verbally that is a deception clue. For example, a person might be expressing concern about something you said. As this occurs, you may notice a very small shrug of the shoulders which conflicts with what the person is saying—the person doesn't really care.

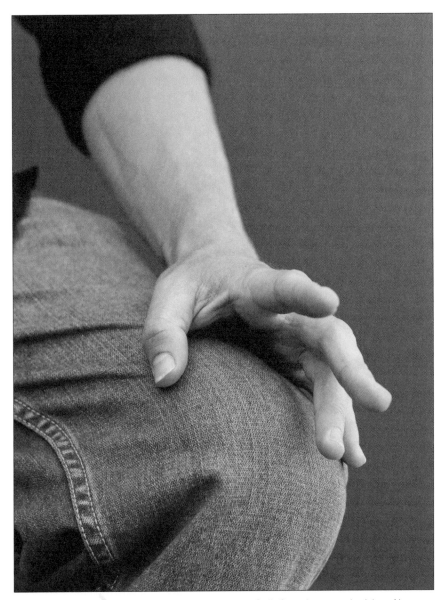

A person starting to fidget or tap fingers during your Guilt Questions may be lying. Also a total lack of movement can indicate deceit—look for movement inconsistency between Control and Guilt Questioning.

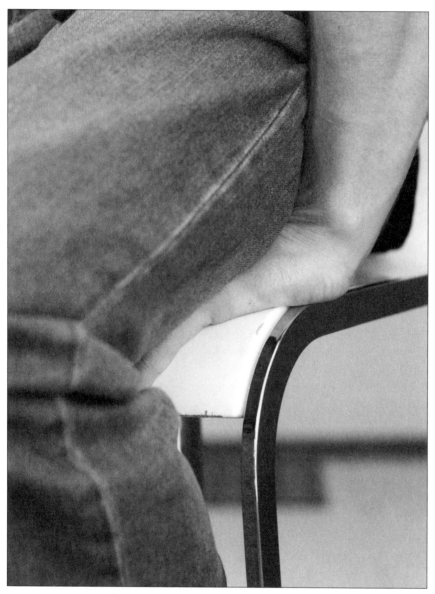

If liars conscious of fidgeting, they may try to hide this by placing their hands in their pockets, under a desk, or clasping them together.

Legs and feet: I believe legs and feet are an underrated source of deception clues and are often missed. Liars are usually acutely aware of arm movement and will minimize it, but forget to reduce the movement in their legs, particularly if they think their legs are hidden out of sight, such as under a table or desk. Similarly to the arms, liars may start to shake one or both legs slightly. To reduce this movement the liar may cross the legs or lock the ankles together. Liars may also use arms or hands to hold against the legs as a kind of brace to minimize movement. Also when seated, liars may spread their legs widely and press their thighs against the arms of the chair to hold them still. Sometimes this is combined with leaning backwards against the back of the chair in an effort to look relaxed, when the liar is anything but. Liars may even feign a yawn when they do this to look disinterested and unconcerned—another giveaway, unless they were yawning during your Control Questions. If so perhaps you need some more interesting Control Questions!

HANDY HINT: The legs provide a great opportunity to observe increased movement. Pay particular attention to the feet and toes if visible, as these will often remain moving even when individuals have locked their ankles or braced their legs against a chair or with their arms. Look for small movements of the feet or legs, as these are hard to control and will give liars away, as they concentrate on controlling arm movement and other more obvious deceit clues.

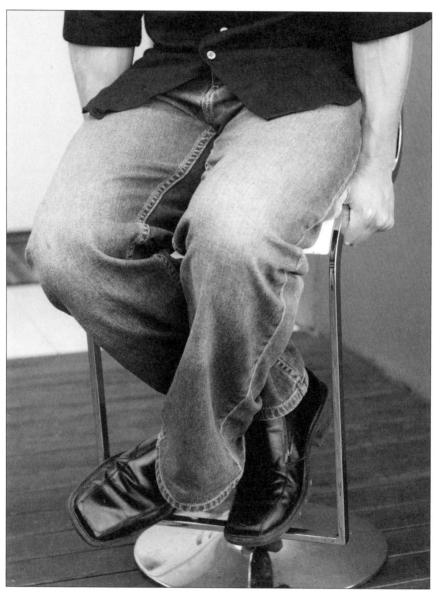

Liars may start to shake one or both legs slightly. To try to hide this, they may cross the legs or lock the ankles.

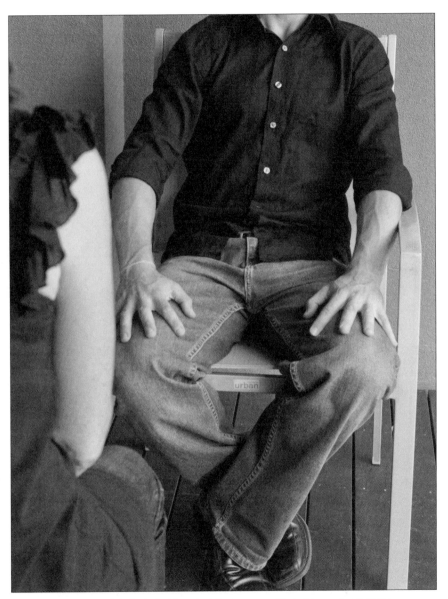

Liars may use arms of chairs to hold against the legs as a kind of brace to minimize movement.

Liars may pretend to be relaxed—a closer inspection reveals the legs are braced against the chair, the fingers are clenched, and the arm is locked into back of the chair.

Head: Often when a person lies, there is a conflict between what is said and what the body demonstrates. When you take the time to observe the movement of the head in particular and listen to what a deceiver is saying, it can become very evident there is a conflict. The person may claim to agree with what you are saying, while shaking the head "no." Similarly, I have seen liars answer verbally "no," while the head nods a positive "yes." This conflict is a good deceit clue.

Posture: When stressed, more often than not, liars will have a closed body posture. They want to take up as little space as possible. To do this, individuals cross their legs, fold their arms, hunch their shoulders, and, if seated, may even slide themselves down the back of the chair slightly. When you ask your Guilt Questions, liars may immediately turn their bodies slightly away from you or adjust their seating position, or they may pretend to be distracted and look in another direction. If the person wasn't doing this before you asked the Guilt Questions, it's a pretty good bet these movements are all deceit clues.

Usually an honest person will display an open and comfortable body posture. Conversely, liars will tend to be stiff and closed and will lean back to distance themselves from the person asking the questions. Liars may even attempt to put an object between themselves and the person asking the question as a comfort or protection barrier. At an office meeting, a barrier could be created by simply raising a folder or some other paperwork to chest level—a good way to hide those telltale deception clues.

Conversely, sometimes in an effort to convey innocence, liars will lean forward (usually combined with increased eye contact) in an effort to convince the person asking the question of the truthfulness of their story, like pushy salesmen would. When doing this, they may also nod their head in rhythm with their speech and if very confident, may even point or tap their finger as they speak. If someone is doing this and trying very hard to convince you of something, check your "Liedar." Innocent people don't try so hard; they expect exoneration.

HANDY HINT: The more people try to convince me of their innocence, the more I suspect them.

If you get a chance, do an Internet search for the video testimony of former president Bill Clinton responding to the Monica Lewinsky scandal, and notice how often he leans forward as an attempt to convince those present of his innocence. A number of these gestures were accompanied by statements that were, to say the least, questionable.

As another counter-measure, liars may deliberately adopt a relaxed posture, opening their arms, spreading their legs, and leaning back. Of course, you will be assessing these movements against the movements you observed when establishing their behavioral baseline: An increase or decrease in activity indicates deception.

HANDY HINT: Liars feel more comfortable telling lies when you can't see them. Ask yourself this question: If you had to tell a significant lie to your boss or some other authoritative figure (i.e., the police), would you prefer to do it on the phone or face-to-face?

The reason people feel more comfortable telling lies without face-to-face contact is because this way, it's easier for them to hide deception clues that could otherwise be given away through body movements to the other person. With this in mind, plan to ask your questions when your subject is standing in plain view, with freedom to move, not seated at a desk where it is possible to anchor to an object (restricting guilty movement) or hide deception clues under a desk or table.

Liars will most likely have a closed body posture to take up as little space as possible. They may cross their legs, fold their arms, hunch their shoulders, and if sitting, even slide themselves down the back of the chair slightly.

When you ask your Guilt Questions, liars may immediately turn their body slightly away from you, adjust their seating position, or pretend to be distracted and look another direction.

Liars tend to be stiff and closed and lean back to distance themselves from the person asking the questions, or even put a barrier or object in front of their body.

Open and relaxed body posture.

Closed body posture—note the hands, arms, and legs are braced to stop movement.

Speaking with forked tongue

As we discussed earlier in the section, *The Nature of Lie Detection: How Good Are We—Naturally?*, Albert Mehrabian's research found that 55 percent of communication was nonverbal (how the body moves), 38 percent was vocal (how things are said) and only 7 percent was purely verbal (what is said).[29] So far, with good reason, we have focused most of our attention on nonverbal signs of lying. In my opinion, nonverbal signs are easier to observe and remember, particularly if you are just starting to develop your lie detection skills. However, given that 45 percent of our communication is conveyed through what words and how words are used, it's worth spending some time looking at deception clues through speech.

Text-bridging: Clever liars prefer to conceal their lies within the truth rather than invent an entire story. One way they do this is by a process called text-bridging. Text-bridging is a process where the person simply "glosses over" parts of a story, which, if told in more detail, would expose a lie. Below is a transcript example of text-bridging. See if you can identify the area of the story the person doesn't want to discuss in detail and is attempting to conceal.

Question: "Tell me in detail what you did this morning."

Answer: "Well, I woke up and had a shower, got dressed, poured myself a coffee, and got the morning paper from the front garden. After I read the paper in the kitchen, I grabbed my car keys and left the house. I saw that my neighbor John Dobbs was leaving for work at the same time; we both took the highway into the city. The traffic was pretty bad, but I still made good time to the city. However, when I got out of the elevator at work, I went to my desk, put my stuff down, turned on my laptop, and started going through some paperwork."

When you read through the answer, you'll notice there is a moderate amount of detail that appears consistently through the account given, except for one glaring hole—the story went from arriving in the city to getting out of the elevator. Where did the person park the car? Considering the amount of detail given as the person went through the morning's activities, it would be reasonable to expect the person would also have mentioned where the car was parked, what happened in the car park, and perhaps what the person saw in the parking lot. However, this has been glossed over in an attempt to conceal an event.

There are some classic text-bridging phrases that you can look for that deceivers commonly use in conversation, such as "the next thing I knew..."; "shortly thereafter..."; "coincidentally..."; "however..."; and "then...."

If you hear any of these in a conversation, it may be the start of a text-bridge being built—over guilty waters. By listening to the amount of detail in a subject's answer, text-bridging will become obvious to you when the subject suddenly jumps from one part of the story to another.

One thing to keep in mind, though, is that a person may appear to be text-bridging when glossing over a certain part of the story, when in reality, the person simply can't be bothered telling you—thinks you may not be interested in the details about that part of the story, or it's not relevant to the point being made. So, if a person is telling you a story, the apparent text-bridging may not necessarily be as a result of lying; the person may simply be protecting you from boring details. Of course, if the person text-bridges more than once around a particular subject an area, this should start your "Liedar" beeping.

Deflection: Deflection is, as the name implies, a way to deflect someone's attention on to something else to avoid being questioned or to avoid answering a question. Liars will sometimes attempt to deflect subtly, usually as part of an overly elaborate answer to a question. Coincidentally, politicians are very good at this technique! The next time you see a politician being grilled by a television reporter about something for which they are clearly guilty or accountable, listen for the deflection as the politician dodges the question and instead focuses the attention on another person, or political party. An example of deflection:

Question: "Why haven't you done more about the traffic congestion by funding more roads, for example?"

Answer: "The problem with traffic congestion is that it is a national matter. In fact, overseas, it's continuously a problem, and with more cars on the road, there are environmental issues to consider. We have put a lot of money into environmental research in an effort to protect the environment and the future for our children."

The slippery politician simply didn't answer the question and deflected the conversation into a subject area in which she/he was well protected. If every time you get close to talking about a suspicious activity and you find the subject has been changed, the person is deflecting to avoid talking about the suspicious activity. "Liedar" on.

People use deflection techniques and text-bridging as a form of protection in regular conversation. Now that you know how to identify these tactics, it can be fun when you hear someone do this as part of a normal conversation, because you have identified there is something the person doesn't want to tell you. While that person may not be lying to you, there is definitely something being hidden. If you are so inclined, you can then menacingly ask questions about the area over which the person has deflected or text-bridged. This is usually met by the person dismissing your question as not important. Yep, something is being hidden.

Even children will adopt this strategy to avoid telling the whole truth. Example:

Child: "Dad, I was in the living room playing my PlayStation with Tracy. I was about to get my highest score, and the next thing I knew, Tracy started hitting me." (*"The next thing I knew." Text-bridging over the incident where Ken took the PlayStation control from Tracy when it was her turn*).

Father: "Did you do something to make her angry?"

Child: "We were just playing. Anyway, Tracy got into trouble with her teacher at school today." (*Deflection to a new area, away from the incident for which the child is guilty*).

Contractions and Overemphasis: Generally, when people lie they avoid using word contractions, such as "I don't," "I wasn't," and "I didn't." A liar will say, "I do not," "I was not," and "I did not." Deceivers may say, "I do not remember" as opposed to "I don't remember," as they are attempting to appear more convincing and very definite in their answer.

Similarly, deceivers sometimes tend to overemphasize their answers with phrases such as, "I would not lie," "I have never lied," or "I was taught never to lie," Additionally, if you hear one of the phrases, "I swear on my mother's life," "to be honest," "to be perfectly frank," "to be perfectly truthful," turn your "Liedar" on, as there is most likely a stream of lies coming your way!

A classic example of overemphasis by Bill Clinton, January 26, 1998:

"Now, I have to go back to work on my State of the Union speech. And I worked on it until pretty late last night. But I want to say one thing to the American people. I want you to listen to me. I'm going to say this again: I did not have sexual relations with that woman, Miss Lewinsky. I never told anybody to lie, not a single time;

never. These allegations are false. And I need to go back to work for the American people. Thank you."[30]

Another way liars overemphasize their story is by providing too much detail in their answers—more than would be expected. They do this to appear more convincing. Like the pushy car salesman who bombards you with car and money details and reasons why you should buy the car, the liar is bombarding you with details in an effort to convince you of his or her innocence. Liars may also do this because they feel that if they give a vague answer, it may be a sign of guilt. So a very detailed answer is simply a counter-strategy.

Regardless of the reason why, if you get an overly elaborate and detailed answer to a question, pursue that area some more. A tactic that works very well with individuals who provide very detailed and elaborate answers is the silent treatment. Ask another question without giving any verbal or behavioral signs of acknowledgment that you believe or disbelieve them. This will place their head in a psychological vice, as they will desperately want feedback from you that you are convinced of their innocence. If you don't provide them with any feedback and remain silent, they will continue to talk in detail, digging themselves further into a hole, as their answer contains more lies and becomes longer and longer. Sometimes, the answers can verge on irrational accounts that have nothing to do with the original question. Sometimes, deceivers will reach the point where they realize that what they have said is totally ridiculous. In a change of tact and in an effort to try to convince you, they may decide to admit that they have been less than truthful—but are now honest (e.g., "Okay, to be perfectly honest with you...") and off they go again with more lies, while you continue to stay silent.

HANDY HINT: Liars will often either ask you to repeat the question you just asked them or they will repeat your question verbally, aloud or sometimes under their breath. This is to give them more thinking time to fabricate a response. When was the last time you were having a normal conversation with a person and you were asked to repeat a question, or the person repeated your question in full? This scenario very rarely occurs under normal circumstances. If this does occur, the person is stalling and using the time to formulate a response. The very sneaky liar will clear his or her throat before responding, again to create time to manufacture falsehoods.

Speech Pattern: When a person is speaking the truth, there is a regular pattern of speech; it flows with a certain rhythm and tone, regardless of what the topic is. Often liars' speech will speed up and slow down during the course of a conversation. Additionally, the tone of their voice may alter between when they are telling the truth and when they are not. Usually, the pitch increases as a result of stress when a person lies.

When people lie, their words slow down as the mind is loaded up (cognitive overload), thinking about what lies have been told previously and how to best lie on this occasion. Conversely, speech will then speed up as the liar talks about matters the mind does not need to manufacture, the truth.

If an individual's speech rapidly increases, this can also be a result of delivering a rehearsed lie that has been practiced or told on many occasions. How do you distinguish between these? You are trying to observe a difference in the speech pattern between the answers to the Control Questions and the Guilt Questions. If the person's speech speeds up or slows down when answering the Guilt Questions, start looking for other signs of deceit.

HANDY HINT: Look for quick yes or no responses, followed by a pause and then a justification of the answer. The liar gives a quick response to the question to avoid appearing guilty, so the answer is delivered quickly, but then the person needs time to fabricate the story.

In addition to changes in speech pattern, liars tend to mispronounce words more regularly than truthful people. If they start to stutter, pause, or mispronounce words in response to your Guilt Questions, this is a fair indication the person is lying.

When challenged verbally, a truthful person will usually be forthcoming with information and be helpful. Truth tellers are confident and expect to be trusted, so their verbal answers are spontaneous, and their speech pattern is fluid and follows a rhythm. Often an innocent person will display some form of resentment towards whoever is responsible, less so toward the person accusing them. When a deceitful person is challenged, he or she is usually less helpful, and the tone of the voice may increase as the speech pattern speeds and slows throughout the conversation. A liar may also become defensive.

Some people will steeple their fingers in front of their face to form an additional barrier—touching their nose and mouth—as Bill Clinton did on several occasions during his Grand Jury testimony. Copyright C-SPAN

Bill Clinton leaning forward giving Grand Jury testimony, he is selling his story to the listener. Politicians and hard-sell salespeople (and pushy people!) do this when "selling" what they are saying—trying to convince others, sometimes when telling the truth, other times when lying. Copyright C-SPAN

Overemphasis—"I'm going to say this again: I did not have sexual relations with that woman, Miss Lewinsky. I never told anybody to lie, not a single time; never." (Press conference January 26, 1998). Copyright C-SPAN

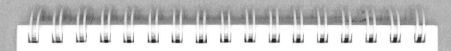

Summary of Main Points

The bullet points below highlight some of the more significant information covered in this section.

Follow the five-step MAGIC Lie Detection Model:

Motivation: Does the person have a motivation to lie?

Ask Control Questions: To establish a behavioral baseline. (Ask Control Questions and observe normal behavior and speech patterns.)

Guilt Questions: Ask Guilt Questions. (Provide the opportunity to lie or tell the truth.)

Indicators: Are there lying indicators occurring in clusters? (Look for inconsistency in behavior and speech patterns, a cluster of lying signs in close succession—in response to your Guilt Questions.)

Check Again: Re-examine. (Ask Control Questions again and then revisit Guilt Questions; if the clue cluster returns, the person is being deceitful.)

The three key areas of the eyes to focus on are: eye contact, blink rate, and eye movement.

When you ask a question, an individual's eyes should:

- Move either horizontally or diagonally upwards—right (your right), if remembering something that actually happened. This indicates to you the person has actually experienced what is being told to you; or,

- Move either horizontally or diagonally upwards—left (your left), if creating something in the mind—something not seen or heard before. This indicates to you the person has not seen or heard what is being told to you.

- The above is for a right-orientated person (right-handed); a left-orientated person (left-handed) will be the opposite.

- You can identify the orientation of a person during your Control Questioning by simply asking about events the person has actually experienced.

- Sometimes a person will look straight ahead with little or no eye movement with the eyes appearing to be unfocused. This is also a sign that the person is recalling an actual event.

- This technique will not work on all people—use it in addition to other lying signs before determining if a person is lying.

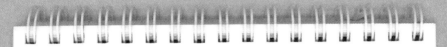

Liars like to cover their mouth, and some will touch their nose either as a method of momentarily covering their mouth with their hand or because the tissues within their nose have become engorged with blood, causing an itching sensation.

A genuine smile affects the muscles around the eyes and takes some time to form and fade. A fake smile is created primarily by the lower half of the face only, and appears and disappears too quickly.

Micro-expressions are involuntary and very fast flashes of emotions on the face. They may appear as a twitch. Regardless of culture, race, or upbringing, the micro-expressions of happiness, sadness, disgust, contempt, anger, surprise, and fear are universal and don't change, so they can be applied to all people.

Micro-expressions are so instantaneous the person expressing them has no control over them. Micro-expressions display the true inner emotion of a person without time to hide it. Look for a conflict between the micro-expressed emotion and the statement made by the person.

Liars will use counter-measures in an attempt to trick you. For example, they may increase the amount of eye contact or reduce the amount of body movement when lying. If this is inconsistent with their behavior when you establish the behavioral baseline, it's a counter-measure, and they are being deceitful.

Liars avoid contractions such as, "I don't," "I wasn't," and "I didn't" and will use, "I do not," "I was not," and "I did not" more often.

Some liars provide overelaborate details in their answer or are pushy, like salesmen, in trying to convince you of their innocence.

Look for inconsistencies in speech pattern and tone. Some classic text-bridging phrases that deceivers commonly use in conversation include: "the next thing I knew…"; "shortly thereafter…"; "coincidentally…"; "however…"; and "then…."

GO FOR IT!

Now that you have read this entire book, if you haven't already, it's time to start practicing. Let the fun begin! The more you practice what is taught in this book the more accurate you will become.

A good place to start testing your skills is on children, as they haven't yet learned to hide their lies very well, and their lying signs are obvious. I also encourage you to practice with friends and family, as they can provide you feedback on when they lied. You can learn a great deal from this.

The tactics taught in this book are not magic tricks, nor are they an exact science. Regardless of your age, gender, language, or cultural background, with practice, you will most definitely improve your accuracy in detecting lies.

Don't be discouraged if your results are not accurate to start with—this is quite often the case. Remember, you are most likely starting with a 45–50 percent accuracy level, but are aiming to be in the 70–80 percent accuracy zone. Even as an accomplished Human Lie Detector, you will miss some lies. I can assure you though, if you correctly apply the information in this book, it will set you on the path to becoming an effective Human Lie Detector—and that's the truth!

Part Three

Easy Reference

THE NATURE OF LYING: SUMMARY OF MAIN POINTS

Lying is a normal part of human communication and should not always be considered a bad thing to do.

People lie regularly, about once every ten minutes during conversation.

Sometimes lying is necessary to protect a person's feelings and to assist with everyday human interaction. On other occasions lying can be very detrimental to people and their relationships.

Other-Focused Lies are directed at another person and are usually told with the good intention of the deceiver. They are sometimes called white lies or good-will lies.

Self-Focused Lies may be directed at any person, but are told for the purpose of benefitting or protecting the person telling the lie. While not always the case, this category of lie can be sinister and damaging.

THE NATURE OF LIE DETECTION: SUMMARY OF MAIN POINTS

Naturally, we are far better at telling lies than detecting them. Without specific training, most people, including those from professions where detecting lies is crucial, achieve a lie-detection rate of about 50 percent.

With specific knowledge (provided by this book) and practice (provided by you), people may achieve a lie-detection rate of 80 percent.

The more you use your "Liedar," the more accurate your lie detection skills will become. However, you don't want it on constantly—knowing when to turn it on will make you more focused when you do use these skills.

There is a special category of Human Lie Detector (referred to as Lie Wizards) that has a natural talent in accurate lie detection without specific training, achieving starting percentages of 80 percent or better.

Most people believe that they can tell if their partner, child, or close friend lies to them. This is usually not the case, due to two primary factors: overconfidence (they know the person well and will therefore be able to see the telltale signs) and closeness (the natural default position for humans is to believe the people they are emotionally close to). These two factors lead to a loss of objectivity, preventing a person in a close relationship from seeing otherwise obvious signs.

Studies have demonstrated that 55 percent of communication is nonverbal (how the body moves/reacts); 38 percent is vocal (how things are said), and only 7 percent is purely verbal (what is said). While what is said cannot be totally discounted in lie detection, how things are said and how a person's body moves/reacts while communicating are far more important.

Relying solely on what is said is inherently unreliable. Accurate lie detectors rely on a combination of what they're told and what they observe.

THE LYING RESPONSE:
SUMMARY OF MAIN POINTS

Broadly speaking, there are three responsive phases after a lie is told:

Phase One: Emotional Response: Recognition by the liar of the falsehood told, which leads to feelings of guilt, fear, stress, and on occasion excitement. How great an impact this will have on the person's behavior is predominantly determined by the magnitude of the consequences of being caught. For example, a small lie will only have a small amount of emotion attached to it. A major deception, such as infidelity, crime, or lying to secure a business contract or employment will usually result in a noticeable increase in these emotions, making them easier to detect.

Phase Two: Sympathetic Nervous Response: The impact of guilt, fear, stress, or excitement on the liar, which results in "deceit clues," such as finger tapping, fidgeting, talking too quickly, avoiding eye contact, and rapid eye movement.

Phase Three: Cognitive Response: A counter-measure attempt by the liar to cover up the "deceit clues." This is more easily done using highly conductive channels (areas of the body over which the liar easily controls, such as hands and eye contact). These areas shouldn't be discounted. However, concentrating on areas with less control such as pupil size, lower body movements, and micro-expressions will be more productive.

The lying response sequence: If the Emotional Response is fear (phase one), and this causes liars to tap their foot (phase two), they will attempt to hide their leg movement (under a table or bracing the legs) to disguise guilt (phase three).

Mentally, we only have $100. Consider that humans have $100 worth of brain capacity at any particular time. Liars need to spend this money carefully to avoid being detected. If they invest too much in hiding deceit clues revealed through body movement, their explanation will not make logical sense. Conversely, if the answer makes sense, they may not have invested enough in hiding guilty body movement. If you ask for further clarification, you may be able to cause mental bankruptcy, revealing an array of obvious deceit clues.

LIE-DETECTION PROCESS—IT'S MAGIC: SUMMARY OF MAIN POINTS

The MAGIC Lie Detection Model is an easy-to-remember process that may be applied to all situations. You may find it helpful to use this summary to refresh your memory. If you would like more detailed information, I suggest you read the entire section titled *Lie-Detection Process—It's MAGIC!*

Motivation: Does the person have a motive to lie? Motivations include: to protect from embarrassment; to make a positive impression; to gain an advantage; and to avoid punishment. You'll be more accurate if you remain objective, so don't assume the person is lying—be aware that the person may have the motivation to lie, but is actually telling the truth.

Ask Control Questions, to establish a baseline: When you initially turn on your "Liedar," observe the verbal and nonverbal responses to Control Questions—ones the person will answer truthfully. This will give you a behavioral baseline. Take your time doing this, as it will create a reliable platform to then detect changes in the person's behavior if he or she is lying.

Guilt Questions: To identify a liar, you need to first provide the opportunity to lie. For this to occur, you must ask a Guilt Question or two—subtly. This is best done as part of a normal conversation, as it denies the opportunity for the person to hide deceit clues from you.

Indicators: Are there lying indicators that stand out to you from the baseline behavior you observed when asking the Control Questions? Did they occur in a clue cluster and in quick succession? When this occurs in response to a guilt question, your "Liedar" should lock on. Some deceit clues are listed at the end of this section.

Check Again: Re-examine. To do this, repeat stages MAGI (above) and validate your observations of the clue cluster. If you observe a similar clue cluster to a previous Guilt Question, it's likely you've caught yourself a liar.

Some Deceit Clues: Finger, hand, leg, or foot movement, or absence of movement; speech pattern changes, increased mispronunciation, throat clearing, exaggerated swallowing, or stuttering; inconsistent eye movement (fabricating not recalling); less eye contact or vastly increased eye contact; itchy nose; closed body posture, leaning back or placing arms across the body to create a barrier; hands in front of mouth or eyes; extended blink followed by a hand to the face; contradictions between "what is said" and "what is gestured" (nodding "yes" but saying "no"); feigning tiredness (e.g., fake yawning); increased embellishment and overly detailed answers; and conflicting micro-expressions.

LYING SIGNS:
SUMMARY OF MAIN POINTS

Follow the five-step MAGIC Lie Detection Model.

The three key areas of the eyes to focus on are: eye contact, blink rate, and eye movement.

When you ask a question, an individual's eyes should:

- Move either horizontally or diagonally upwards—right (your right), if remembering something that actually happened. This indicates to you the person has actually experienced what is being told to you; or,

- Move either horizontally or diagonally upwards—left (your left), if creating something in the mind—something not seen or heard before. This indicates to you the person has not seen or heard what is being told to you.

- The above is for a right-orientated person (right-handed); a left-orientated person (left-handed) will be the opposite.

- You can identify the orientation of a person during your Control Questioning by simply asking about events the person has actually experienced.

- Sometimes a person will look straight ahead with little or no eye movement with the eyes appearing to be unfocused. This is also a sign that the person is recalling an actual event.

- This technique will not work on all people—use it in addition to other lying signs before determining if a person is lying.

Liars like to cover their mouth, and some will touch their nose either as a method of momentarily covering their mouth with their hand or because the tissues within their nose have become engorged with blood, causing an itching sensation.

A genuine smile affects the muscles around the eyes and takes some time to form and fade. A fake smile is created primarily by the lower half of the face only, and appears and disappears too quickly.

Micro-expressions are involuntary and very fast flashes of emotions on the face. They may appear as a twitch. Regardless of culture, race, or upbringing, the micro-expressions of happiness, sadness, disgust, contempt, anger, surprise, and fear are universal and don't change, so they can be applied to all people.

Micro-expressions are so instantaneous the person expressing them has no control over them. Micro-expressions display the true inner emotion of a person without time to hide it. Look for a conflict between the micro-expressed emotion and the statement made by the person.

Liars will use counter-measures in an attempt to trick you. For example, they may increase the amount of eye contact or reduce the amount of body movement when lying. If this is inconsistent with their behavior when you establish the behavioral baseline, it's a counter-measure, and they are being deceitful.

Liars avoid contractions such as, "I don't," "I wasn't," and "I didn't" and will use, "I do not," "I was not," and "I did not" more often.

Some liars provide overelaborate details in their answer or are pushy, like salesmen, in trying to convince you of their innocence.

Look for inconsistencies in speech pattern and tone. Some classic text-bridging phrases that deceivers commonly use in conversation include: "the next thing I knew..."; "shortly thereafter..."; "coincidentally..."; "however..."; and "then...."

LYING SIGNS: EASY REFERENCE LIST

As mentioned throughout this book, lying signs observed during the Guilt Questions need to be compared against the same signs and behaviors the subject demonstrated during the Control Questions. What you are looking for is an inconsistency between the two. Some lying signs will increase, indicating a person is lying, and some will decrease as the person attempts to disguise guilt. For example, one liar will increase movement when asked questions, but another will sit rigid like a statue as an attempt to hide guilt. Inconsistency is the key. Look for:

- Finger, hand, leg, and/or foot movement, or unnatural absence of movement.
- Speech pattern changes—changing the tense between or within sentences.
- Mispronunciation.
- Speech doesn't flow smoothly and naturally.
- Repeating the question—cognitive overload—liar needs more time to fabricate.
- Inconsistent eye movement, fabricating not recalling.
- Avoiding or forcing eye contact.
- Blinking slows or increases.
- Dry lips.
- Less color in lips.
- Itchy nose—due to increased blood flow to erectile tissues.
- Creates a barrier.
- Hands, arms, legs crossed.
- Body movements are jerky—not relaxed and natural.
- Pursed lips.

- Hands in front of mouth or eyes.
- Hand on chin, finger reaching up to edge of the mouth.
- No hand-steepling, or hand-steepling in front of the face.
- Throat clearing.
- Deep swallowing.
- Stuttering.
- Pupils dilate.
- Contradictions between what is said and what is gestured.
- Feigning tiredness (e.g., fake yawning).
- Insincere smiling.
- Clipped or shallow breathing, faster breathing.
- Micro-expression conflicts with what is said (i.e., liar says, "Happy to see you," but micro-expression shows "disgust").
- Extended blink, followed by hand to face.
- Withdrawn or closed body posture, or suspiciously open body posture.
- Text-bridging in sentence construction.
- Lack of speech contractions.
- Overly elaborate and detailed answers.

LYING SIGNS:
IMAGE REFERENCE GUIDE

Increased eye contact.

Looking away.

Raising hands in front of face.

Rubbing eyes and looking away.

Looking to the left: creating or fabricating.

Looking to the right: recalling a real event.

Checking to see if lie was accepted.

Frequent nose touching.

Holding mouth closed or pinching lips.

Covering mouth with hands. Turning away.

Covering mouth with pen or object.

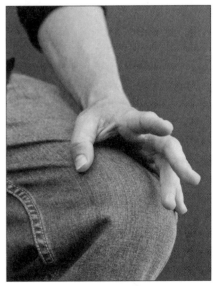

Finger, hand, leg movement.

Hiding hands to control fidgeting.

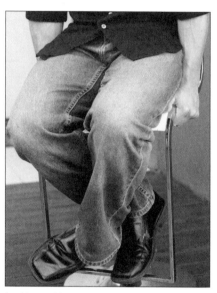

Locking ankles to control shaking.

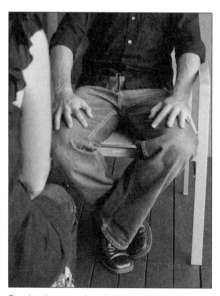

Bracing legs against a chair to minimize movement.

Pretending to be relaxed.

Turning body away. Adjusting position.

Using an object to create distance.

Showing closed body language.

MICRO-EXPRESSIONS: IMAGE REFERENCE GUIDE

Happiness.

Sadness.

Anger.

Contempt.

Disgust.

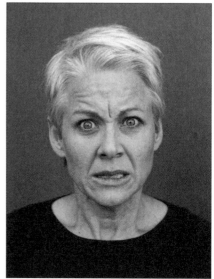

Fear.

Surprise.

HANDY HINTS—
PARENTS AND TEACHERS

Some may feel that questioning children using these methods is not a fair activity—that it invades their privacy. However, I believe that in the correct circumstances, knowing the truth is essential for a child's welfare and is a value that should be taught by parents and teachers. I don't advocate always testing children for the truth, just when it really matters. Remember to always apply the MAGIC Model. Here are some helpful precautions to take before questioning a child to determine lies:

Question Commensurate to the child's age: How intensely you go about questioning a child should be strictly governed by the age of the child. For example, your questioning may be quite vigorous with a seventeen-year-old, but gentle with an eight-year-old. Also, remember that young children around five years of age may not yet have developed the capacity to lie and may not be lying; they may be simply just telling you about their imagination. When she was four, one of my daughters told me "honestly" that a spider broke our sprinkler. Factually, it was a lie, but she truly she believed what she had said. You can't chastise a child for this, so be careful not to punish a genuine imagination. Additionally, if you push a child too hard during questioning, they'll admit to most things regardless of whether they are guilty or not, or along the same lines, they will just tell you what they think you want to hear. This is exacerbated where there is a clear difference in the power dynamics of the relationship, as would be the case where a school principal questions a child, compared to a young student teacher questioning the same child. Accurate lie detection is about identifying the truth—not coercing an innocent. It's more accurate and more fair to question carefully and appropriately to the child's age.

Beware of Overconfidence and Remain Objective: For parents, questioning your own children is always a tricky endeavor, as parents are naturally biased by our closeness with and confidence in them, as discussed earlier in the book. Depending on how much you love the little terror and your natural presumption of knowledge, you may miss deceit clues. Deciding whether they are lying or telling the truth before making a proper assessment (using MAGIC) will only lead to an inaccurate conclusion. In the case of teachers, it's equally important not to base your lie detection upon a student's history. A student that has lied often in the past may not do so on all occasions. Conversely, the ideal "butter wouldn't melt in my mouth" student will, on occasion, lie. It's not easy to remain impartial, particularly if you already suspect a child of some misbehavior or presume a child is innocent. To increase your accuracy on each occasion, the approach needs to be judicious and one where you question carefully and impartially applying the MAGIC Model.

The Body of a Child Yells: For the tricky child subject, I recommend asking your questions while the child is standing. The reason for this is that children have less muscular control in the face and body than adults do. So, when using the MAGIC Model and then changing from Control Questions to Guilt Questions, the guilty child will move incongruently with previous movements when answering truthfully. Children's movements are vastly exaggerated in these circumstances, so you can use that to your advantage.

Pros and Cons of Bluffing: Some parents and teachers may try to convince children they are questioning that they can always tell when they are lying. This method works quite effectively, until you get it wrong, in which case the child has found you out and therefore you simply will lose credibility and their respect. Remember that without training, lie detection accuracy is around 50 percent, and that even with training and knowledge, the highest accuracy most people can expect to reach is about 80 percent. The MAGIC Model is not infallible, so if you catch a child lying once, don't claim that you can do it every time, because you can't (I can't either)—you can let them think it, though. Implicit bluffing is more effective and has a longer effective time range.

EXAMPLE: I distinctly remember breaking my younger brother's bike when I was about seven, and thought no one knew—but Dad did, and I got into trouble fair and square. "How did you know?" I asked (not knowing the neighbor had told him), and all he said was, "Sometimes, dads know these things." From that answer, I remember thinking that Dad could read my mind, so in future I very rarely told him lies. If Dad had called me out every time he thought I was lying, eventually he would have been wrong and I would have discovered his lie, and this discovery would have freed me up to lie again at will. However, not knowing when he knew and when he didn't was a somewhat tortuous way of ensuring I would tell the truth always. I suggest that you apply a similar strategy with your children or students. If you catch the child lying, saying, "Moms sometimes know these types of things" is far better than saying, "I can always tell when you lie" or, "a little bird told me." That will just make the child hate birds!

Learn from Their Lying: For parents, one of the best ways to learn your child's deceit clues is to be patient and study their behavior. Don't wait until there is a critical issue at hand and then try to use your skills—this won't be reliable. My advice is to wait until there is an opportunity to learn something about your child's misbehavior through another means, other than MAGIC. It must be reliable information, the child is confident you don't know. For example, if another parent or a teacher informs you that your pride and joy was caught cheating on a test at school, use that accurate information, and then apply the MAGIC Model. When you ask the Guilt Questions, observe the child's deceit clues—they will definitely be there. Store these in your mind for future reference. Don't reveal that you know she/he lied. If the child believes he or she got away with it on that occasion, the child will naturally revert to the same method next time. When there is a critical issue, you can again apply MAGIC and see if the same or similar signs manifest. This will be more reliable.

A Final Note: Parents, remember lie detection of your own child, particularly when they are older, is one of the hardest things to do correctly. Getting it wrong can be very hurtful, so please tread carefully. Teachers, having so many children to deal with makes your task particularly hard; you simply cannot and should not try to learn all of your students' deceit clues. Remember, a student's antecedence (positive or negative) is the greatest threat to your accuracy, so only turn your "Liedar" on when you really need to, and approach each situation impartially.

Most obvious deceit clues from children:

Eyes: Observe the eyes: these will flit around the room and look everywhere except where your eyes are; this is more obvious in younger children. Also observe the eye movement; is the child actually recalling something or searching the mind for ideas to invent answers? (See the section in the book on *Eye Movements* on page 62.)

Fidgeting or Playing with an Object: This habit tends to be more prominent in children over seven years of age and is a natural distraction tool. Children do this so they don't have to look at you; it's as if they are too busy. It's a step up in sophistication from younger children who simply look about the room anywhere except where the parent is.

Hand to Mouth: The younger the child, the more obvious this gesture will be. A young child may place the entire hand over the mouth—trying to cover where the lie came from. Older children will be more subtle, but may still raise their hands to their faces or attempt to hide their faces from you momentarily by getting a glass of water (averting your gaze while doing so) and then using the glass to hide their mouth as they drink.

Speech Pattern: This sign is more prominent in younger children—their speech will slow right down while they think of something to fabricate (due to an increase in cognitive load), and then speed up as they deliver the fabricated reply (to make up for the "guilty" time delay). Teenagers also do this, but more subtly. Teenagers will also use verbal distraction, such as changing the subject abruptly, asking you a question without answering yours, or pointing out something totally irrelevant to the subject at hand. An overly detailed or elaborate answer is a dead surefire deceit giveaway, especially if the teenager is usually very brief in their truthful responses.

Use the Silent Treatment: If the child answers you, and you're not sure if it is the truth or not, pause—wait, look, and fix your eyes on him or her. Don't show any expression; the latter is the most important as the guilty child will either be looking at other things constantly, unwilling to look back at you, or, if the child is older, glance briefly at you to see if the lie was believed. In both cases, the child will be desperate for information from you on whether you were deceived or not. No answer and no expression increases pressure on the guilty mind. The child will most likely say, "What?" seeking any sort of feedback possible, or may rephrase the answer, making it more detailed and more convincing. Guilty, your honor.

HANDY HINTS— RECRUITMENT INTERVIEWING AND NEGOTIATION

Recruitment, interviewing, and negotiation are subjects in their own right that have numerous elements and factors to consider to be conducted successfully. While there are no specific deceit clues that only occur during interviews and negotiation, this Handy Hints section deals with some techniques that assist in identifying deceit in these situations. While the job applicant and the negotiator may come to the table from differing perspectives and also have a different relationship with you—the former usually the lesser of the two—there are certain tactics applicable to both that may assist you in identifying deceit. For this reason, I've included them in this Handy Hints section. Remember to always apply the MAGIC Model.

Nervous is Normal: We have discussed several deceit clues, some of which become more prevalent when a person is nervous, such as dry lips, closed body posture, and deep swallowing. Under normal circumstances when these types of clues are revealed during the Guilt Questioning phase, they indicate deceit. The situation of the negotiator and the interviewee is slightly different, as both may commence their interaction with you already in a nervous state, and then relax as the process continues. As such, if you apply the MAGIC Model from the outset, your Control Questions may be asked of a nervous person, and you will observe this baseline behavior as being truthful. By the time you move to asking your Guilt Questions, the person may feel more comfortable in the environment and appear to be answering truthfully, when in fact the person is not. The best way to counteract this situation is to take your time. Acknowledge the person may be nervous, and allow some time to settle. There is plenty of time during negotiations and interviews to identify deceit, but to do so more accurately, it is critical to establish a reliable and truthful baseline. To help the person settle, ask simple questions or discuss matters off the topic you intend to ask—talk about the weather, traffic, or coffee. Once the person has settled, commence your Control Questions and establish a reliable baseline from which you may then identify deceit clues during the Guilt Questioning.

Setting the Environment: During interviews and negotiations, there are some environmental factors that you can utilize to your advantage that will assist you in identifying deceit. You may recall from earlier in the book that due to the Sympathetic Nervous Response (the "fight or flight" reaction), liars naturally want to move their bodies more, such as adjusting their seating position or moving their legs and tapping their fingers. Therefore, liars will attempt to control or hide these movements as a counter-strategy (Cognitive Response) to disguise guilt. This being the case, you can "counter this counter-strategy" by making it harder for them to hide guilty movements. The following are some simple and effective measures that make it more difficult to hide guilty movements: arranging for the other party to sit on a swivel chair; having their chair positioned slightly lower than yours; arranging the office so you can observe their lower body movements (remembering that less conductive channels are harder for liars to control—feet and toes fall into this category); and having items on the desk they may easily choose to pick up, such as a pen or eraser. All of these measures are aimed at providing them with as much freedom of movement as possible. This way when you are asking your Guilt Questions, such as, "Were you fired from your last job?" or, "Is that the highest offer your company can make?" and the person lies, the guilty movements will be amplified, making them easier for you to spot.

Text-bridging and Distraction: As mentioned earlier in the book, text-bridging is a process where a person simply "glosses over" parts of a story which, if told in more detail, would expose a lie. Sometimes during interviews and negotiations, text-bridging is followed directly by a distraction aimed at diverting a person's attention away from the area that has been avoided by the deceiver. When an interviewee or negotiator does this, it indicates a weakness and is cause for further exploration of the details you may wish to explore more fully, because something is probably being hidden from you. It may be a gap in the person's employment history, or in the case of a negotiator it may indicate a vulnerability in the capacity to deliver a certain outcome or timeframe.

An example: Applicant for Magee's Gym.

Interviewer: "Could you please outline your recent work experience?"

Interviewee: "I worked for thirteen months at Woodgate's Gym and Fitness Center, where I ran all the aerobic classes and circuit training for three days of the week. On the other days, I assisted with administration, so I have good experience in both areas of the business. After they closed the gym, I worked at Ashby's Gym for a while, and now I'm really keen to get started at Magee's Gym in any area you need help in—administration, instruction, personal training. I'm a very motivated person."

Can you identify the area this person doesn't want examined—where has the person text-bridged, and is there a subtle distraction? When you read the answer, you notice there is a great deal of detail around the applicant's time at Woodgate's Gym and Fitness Center, then the information becomes vague around Ashby's Gym (text-bridge). Right after, the details increase again (the distraction) when the applicant speaks of the new job. I would advise the interviewer to ask more questions about Ashby's Gym, or perhaps phone them for a reference.

A similar example can occur during a negotiation process, where the other party glosses over a particular aspect and/or attempts to distract you from some aspect of the deal, so be alert to these techniques—they're a warning sign for you. Text-bridging and distraction alone don't indicate deceit, but knowing what they are makes it easier to identify places where you should increase your focus.

Friendly, Friendly, Hard Technique: Asking the right questions during interviews and negotiations is one critical factor towards achieving a successful outcome. To assist in identifying deceit during these processes, a good technique is to ask a question that unexpectedly puts the other person on the spot. When this occurs, truthful people recover quickly; liars on the other hand will have that "deer caught in the headlights" look and leak deceit clues as they stumble with a verbal response—due to the sudden increase in cognitive load. To maximize the impact of these questions, timing becomes important. I employ a "friendly, friendly, hard" approach. This approach leads people down a "friendly" path, disarming them, and then all of a sudden the "hard" question is thrown at them. For truthful people, this is no problem, as they simply default back to truthful information they already have. For liars, they need to very quickly invent information that, due to the friendly path they have been walked down, they have not had time to prepare. This will cause the liar to leak more obvious deceit clues. For added impact, when you ask the hard question, lock your eyes directly onto the person it is aimed at.

An important thing to remember when you use this technique is to avoid asking a double-barrelled hard question; in other words, one that is made up of two parts. These types of questions give people a choice as to which part of the question they can answer, and with hard questions, you do not want to make this option available to them. An example of a doubled-barrelled question: "Is this your best price, and is the product good quality?" In response to this, the person can reply by talking about the quality of the product, but avoid answering a direct question about price.

"Friendly, Friendly, Hard" example:

Q: "If we agree to purchase these, you can deliver them on time?"
A: "Yes."

Q: "You've been providing these for several years?"
A: "Yes."

Q: "And there's good after-sales service?"
A: "Yes."

Q: "And your best price is $1200?"
A: "Yes."

Q: "Why can't you make the price cheaper?" (Single-barrel, hard question)

The final question will force the person to either answer truthfully, or quickly invent, reasons to substantiate the price. It may make honest people uncomfortable but they'll recover quickly. For the liar, it will take some considerable mental effort and time to regain composure, and unless the person has practiced this lie often in the past, he or she will be swimming in deceit clues.

A Final Note: Regardless of whether you are interviewing a senior executive or a laborer, negotiating a deal on a washing machine or a multimillion-dollar contract, the successful detection of deceit can save you both money and heartache. As there are no specific deceit clues that only occur during interviews and negotiations, in order to safeguard your interests from deceit as often and effectively as possible, I recommend reading this entire book and then combining the suggestions in the Handy Hints pages with the process of the MAGIC Model.

REFERENCED MATERIAL AND ENDNOTES

1. Dr. Paul Ekman in "How to Spot a Liar" by James Geary, www.time.com/time/world/article/0,8599,205 1177,00.html. See Caveat in this book stating limitations in lie detection accuracy.

2. University of Massachusetts study quoted in The College of St. Scholastica article, "Lying and Deception" at http://faculty.css.edu/dswenson/web/OB/lying.html. Also psychologist Gerald Jellison (University of South California) found that people are lied to approximately one untruth every five minutes in "How to Spot a Liar" by James Geary www.time.com/time/world/article/0,8599,2051177,00.html; Dr. Charles Ford, author of *Lies! Lies!! Lies!!!,* says that the average Joe lies seven times an hour—if you count all the times people lie to themselves. Dr. Ford is a psychiatrist and professor at the University of Alabama at Birmingham. www.nlag.net/Sermons/Transcripts/mjdeadmendont.htm.

3. Feldman, R. S. Forrest, J. A. and Happ, B. R. (2002) *Self Presentation and Verbal Deception: Do Self Presenters Live More?*

4. According to Professor Bella Paulo's research conducted at the University of Massachusetts in 1996.

5. According to Professor Bella Paulo's research conducted at the University of Massachusetts in 1996.

6. "Why Don't We Catch Liars;" Paul Ekman in *Social Research volume* 63, 1996.

7. Ekman, P. (2001) *Telling Lies.*

8. Some research has shown that people from a deprived background or broken home have an increased ability to detect and tell lies. However, there is also contrary research to this finding.

9. "Why Don't We Catch Liars;" Paul Ekman in *Social Research volume* 63, 1996.

10. Ekman and O'Sullivan, 1991; DePaulo and Pfeiffer, 1986. The only category that attained a high level were members of the US Secret Service reaching 80 percent accuracy.

11. Kraut and Poe (1980) "Humans as Lie Detectors: some second thoughts." *Journal of Communication,* 30, pages 209–216. See also Kraut, R. E., and Poe, D. (1980). "Behavioral Roots of Person Perception: The Deception Judgments of Customs Inspectors and Laymen." *Journal of Personality and Social Psychology* 39, 784-798. Police and also customs officers in many countries now receive additional training, which should improve upon the results found in this study.

12. "Who Can Catch a Liar?" Ekman and O'Sullivan (1991), *American Psychologist* 46 pages 913-920.

13. "A Few Can Catch a Liar"; Ekman, O'Sullivan and Frank (1999). *American Psychological Society* 10, No 3.

14. Anthropologist Ray Birdwhistell found similar results.

15. "A Few Can Catch a Liar"; Ekman, O'Sullivan and Frank (1999). *American Psychological Society* 10, No 3.

16. A study by Dr. Maureen O'Sullivan PhD (Lie Wizard Project) at the University of San Francisco found thirty-one wizards among 13,000 people tested.

17. Though there are some limitations in that Doctor O'Sullivan found that all Lie Wizards were intelligent.

18. Article by Gregory A. Perez, "'Wizards' Can Spot the Signs of a Liar: A Rare Few Have the Skill to Detect the Flickers of Falsehood, Scientists Say," quoting the findings of Doctor Maureen O'Sullivan, *at* www. msnbc.msn.com/id/6249749.

19. Having said that, nothing in this subject area is 100 percent, so you will need to apply your own personal judgement as to how you use the results of the lie detection. As previously said, armed with the requisite knowledge and practice, your lie detection will be more accurate than that of the average person.

20. Littlepage, G. E. and Pinealut, M. A. (1985). "Detection of Deception of Planned and Spontaneous Communications." *The Journal of Social Psychology* 125(2), 195-201.

21. *Analysis of Blink Rate Patterns in Normal Subjects*, Bentivoglio AR, Bressman SB, Cassetta E, Carretta D, Tonali P, Albanese A at Istituto di Neurologia, Università Cattolica del Sacro Cuore, Rome, Italy. www. ncbi.nlm.nih.gov/pubmed/9399231.

22. *Frogs into Princes*, Neuro Linguistic Programming by Richard Bandler and John Grinder, Published by Real People Press/UT in 1979.

23. Based on the work by Doctor Alan Hirsch and Doctor Charles Wolf. See also, "Gestures reveal what the lips conceal. (Literature on Mendacity)," www.thefreelibrary.com/ Gestures+reveal+what+the+lips+conceal.+(Literature+on+Mendacity).-a085408941.

24. President Clinton's Grand Jury Testimony of August 17, 1998.

25. About once every four minutes. The author of this book does not assert in any way that former US president Bill Clinton is a deceitful person; this book relies upon the findings in academically published articles and published reports that have examined the subject Grand Jury Testimony.

26. Peter Collett, author of *The Book of Tells*, published by Random House.

27. Information on training can be found at www.paulekman.com/.

28. Based on the research by Dr. Paul Ekman.

29. Anthropologist Ray Birdwhistell found similar results.

30. http://millercenter.org/scripps/archive/speeches/detail/3930.

About the Author

Dr. David Craig achieved his doctorate in law by completing international research of undercover programs in Australia, the United States, Canada, the United Kingdom, and the Netherlands.

Knowing when people tell the truth and when they lie can be a matter of life and death in the world of undercover work; this was the birthplace for *Detect Deceit*.

Dr. Craig has used the techniques in this book extensively and been published in Australia and overseas.

In addition to having over twenty years of criminological experience and research focused on deception and deception detection, Dr. Craig has spent many hundreds of hours researching the theoretical work of some of the world's finest academics on this subject to produce *Detect Deceit*, a practical and easy-to-read book with appeal in the areas of law enforcement, education, parenting, relationships, and business.